ADVANCED GRANT WRITING FOR FEMALE FOUNDERS

Seek and Secure $100,000 or more in funding

LISA ERHART

FOUNDER FUNDING4GROWTH

Published by:
Lisa Erhart, Sydney, Australia
funding4growth.io
© Lisa Erhart, 2024. All rights reserved.

For permission requests, contact the publisher at lisa@funding4growth.io
Cover design by Hazel Lam

Paperback - ISBN: 978-0-6459762-0-5
eBook - ISBN: 978-0-6459762-1-2

Disclaimer
The material in this publication is offered for the general benefit of entrepreneurs
who identify as women but may also be relevant to those considered a minority in the
entrepreneurial ecosystem. It is not intended as professional advice, nor does it provide
specific guidance for particular circumstances, and it should not be relied on as the basis
for any decision to take action or not take action on any matter that it covers. Readers
should obtain professional advice, where appropriate, before making any such decision. To
the maximum extent permitted by law, the author and publisher disclaim all responsibility
and liability to any person or entity arising directly or indirectly from any person or
entity taking or not taking action based on the information in this publication.

The information given in this book should not be treated as a substitute for legal,
financial or other professional advice and should never be used in replacement of such.
The publisher and the author do not make any guarantees as to results that may be
obtained from using the contents of this book. Case studies or references provided in
this book are independent and genuine but do not represent a guarantee or warranty of
similar results.

"Ideas, even million-dollar ones, are most vulnerable in their infancy; don't share them with too many people. However, don't hide your plan from people who can help you move it forward."

SARA BLAKELY

Thank You for being a guiding light for women entrepreneurs globally!
xo

ACKNOWLEDGEMENT OF COUNTRY - AUSTRALIA AND NEW ZEALAND

I am deeply grateful for the sacrifices made by others who have paved the way for the privileges I enjoy today.

In writing this book, I am mindful that I do so on the ancestral lands of the First Nations People of Australia and the Māori people of Aotearoa New Zealand. In the spirit of appreciation, I pay my respects to the Traditional Custodians of these countries and honour their enduring connections to the land, sea, and community.

I extend my heartfelt respect to the Elders, both past and present, and to all Aboriginal and Torres Strait Islander, and Tangata Whenua peoples who contribute to the vibrancy and richness of these nations.

In particular, I wish to recognise the Gadigal people and Ngāi Tahu who have stewarded these lands for generations. Their enduring wisdom and cultural heritage are woven into the very fabric of place, and I am humbled to be able to share my work from this sacred spaces.

GENDER AND IDENTITY

In recognising the diverse tapestry of entrepreneurs seeking funding, I want to extend my heartfelt support to all underrepresented individuals facing challenges in securing the resources they rightfully deserve.

While the term female is used in the pages of this book, it has been used for practical purposes, with the aim to assist readers in navigating relevant search terms for grant research. I want to emphasise that the information within these pages also holds significance for you. My humble request is this: whenever you encounter the term female, please substitute it with the gender identity that resonates with you.

As you embark on your quest for grant opportunities, I encourage you to research for opportunities using terminology that authentically mirrors your identity and aligns with the goals of your project. Your unique perspective and experiences are invaluable, and I want to ensure that you feel seen and included in this journey.

Contents

This is Not the End   195

INTRODUCTION

Trillions of dollars available and how much is secured by women entrepreneurs?

It is hard to comprehend just how much funding is available worldwide on any given day. No one knows *precisely* how much it is, but here's what we do know.

In 2021/2022, the UK government offered GBP 172.1 billion in grant funding[1]. For the financial year 2022, the US government allocated USD 1.2 trillion in financial assistance, and the amount of venture capital invested in US businesses was USD 345 billion. Add to that the total value of publicly traded stocks in the open market in 2022, valued at USD 101.2 trillion, and it is fair to say there is *a significant amount of money* flowing from those who have it to those who want it.

Why should you care?

As a woman and an entrepreneur, it is essential that you take a moment to digest just how much external funding potential there is. I want you to breathe it in. The magnitude of these numbers is mind-blowing.

---

1 Source: UK Parliament House of Commons, research briefing, Government Grants Statistics, June 2023

The mortifying part of this story? It's regularly reported that women receive less than 4%[2] of available funding. Here's the thing …

We know women create businesses that:

- Are more impact focused;
- Carry less debt and, therefore, less risk; and
- Turn every $1 received in funding into an additional 78 cents in revenue (in comparison to the 31 cents additional revenue in businesses run solely by men)[3].

Good things come when women receive the funding they are seeking. For example, greater inclusivity and diverse employment opportunities result from internal policies that reflect real–world issues such as paid menstrual leave, fertility treatment leave, and transition leave. Everyone benefits when women create wealth for themselves, using business as a mechanism.

Now, I don't share information about the size of the global funding pool to dwarf you or your business. Instead, I want you to shift your perspective – just a little – to consider a new way of thinking.

Money is everywhere.

Isn't it fascinating to learn there is more money available than you ever thought possible? If it is changing hands, moving from one entity (a funder) to another entity (a business), then why is it bypassing your business?

If we haven't met before, my name is Lisa Erhart. I am a funding specialist and the founder of Funding4Growth. I am the successful

---

2 The 4% figure used here is a middle of the road statistic because this statistic depends on so many factors, such as your country of residence, country of birth, type of business, heritage, sexual orientation and more... I've seen some statistics less than 1% and others as high as 8%. It's ridiculous to even refer to 8% as 'high'!

3 As reported by the Boston Consulting Group in partnership with Mass Challenge, https://www.bcg.com/publications/2018/why-women-owned-startups-are-better-bet

recipient of more than $4.2 million in funding and an invited assessor for funded accelerator programs and government grants.

I am taking my experiences and turning them into opportunities to teach. I help women entrepreneurs like you bridge the gap between bootstrapping their business growth and tapping into the trillions of dollars available to accelerate that growth.

I'm here to help you to step into the flow of all that money. Whether you take action or not, money will continue flowing from one recipient to another. Therefore, my question is this: how can you position yourself to ensure some of it comes your way?

Even though I'd love a crystal ball, I don't have one, so I've made a few assumptions about you, my courageous reader. Given that you were inspired to pick up this book, I assume that you likely fit into one of the following categories:

- You've previously applied/pitched for funding but have consistently failed;
- You've successfully secured small funding amounts, such as $5k or $10k grants, but now you're ready to level-up by applying for much more significant amounts; or
- You've never considered applying for grants, but you're beginning to see the untapped potential in this often overlooked opportunity.

I've also taken the liberty to assume you don't mind me talking in Australian dollars, as that's the context of my experience and from where I'm writing this book. As such, I'm referring to AUD, where you see the $ sign. All other currencies are noted with the currency code as we go. For example, where the quoted research comes out of the US, as in the case of the World Bank, I'll be sure to make clear that I'm talking about USD.

The action of applying for funding is one part of the process, but it's not the beginning. Being aware of available funding is a critical first step.

In addition to the principles you'll learn in this book, I've created a YouTube channel to profile funding opportunities that I come across. It was set up with the intention that you'll use this awareness to position yourself and your business so that you can access the external funding you're looking for to help grow your impact and your legacy.

If you haven't already, be sure to subscribe to my channel @Funding4Growth and stay informed as new videos are uploaded.

By helping you understand grants as a product in the funding ecosystem, I hope you'll transfer the learnings from this book into other opportunities such as accelerator applications, competition or award submissions, and maybe even partnership proposals.

Much of what is included in this book is transferable and relevant to other parts of your business. My request of you this that you simply keep an open mind, believe that anything is possible, and see what opportunities float to the surface for your attention.

In the meantime, I very much look forward to playing my part in helping you succeed!

A PERSONAL NOTE ...

Hello! I am so very pleased you're here

By reading this book, you are joining a growing movement of purpose-driven founders focused on securing funding to grow legacy businesses with long-term impact and financial sustainability.

I aim to bridge the funding gap separating overlooked and underfunded founders from our well-resourced counterparts. In my experience, there is little that differentiates the underlying fundamentals of businesses led by *minority* founders. Isn't it ridiculous that women are considered a minority in this space!

When business-savvy entrepreneurs (aka *women*) are securing less than 4% of the funding available, an undeniable problem urgently needs addressing.

This book, *Advanced Grant Writing for Female Founders*, will focus on getting you funded. You have in your hands incredible information and insight that will guide you step by step through the entire funding process, from go to whoa. With this book, you benefit from my (*many*) years of experience in grants and capital investment. It is designed to fast-track your ability to secure the funds you need to grow a long-term, financially sustainable business.

I'm here to help you up-skill and start applying for available funds ASAP!

What this book does differently

The structure of *Advanced Grant Writing for Female Founders* is unlike anything you'll find in bookstores or online.

Big statement, I know. But it's true.

I can 100% guarantee that no one else in the world will have prepared a book with this unique blend of knowledge, tools, and resources.

It has taken me years to collate this information and it is definately worth the wait!

Structured in a way that gets you taking action immediately, you will walk away confident about implementing what you've learned. This book is presented in four parts:

1. Dissecting a grant program and/or funding opportunity;
2. Preparing your draft application;
3. Reviewing your draft objectively through the eyes of an assessor; and
4. Reworking your application into a powerful final draft.

Sounds simple ...

... but is it?

If applying for $100k or more via grant opportunities was easy, more (*many more*) women entrepreneurs would be successfully growing their businesses with this type of capital injection. But the reality is they aren't. When I assess grant applications seeking $100k or more in funding, I'm thrilled if I see as many as 20% of the applications for assessment from females.

As thrilled as I am it is still not enough, but 20% is better than it was. In years gone by I would get excited to see just one woman applicant in the mix of applications I was assessing. Even though we're moving in the right direction, it is time to kick into turbo mode and secure a more even share.

I know that day is coming. I can feel it in my bones!

I hope you are among them.

MAXIMISING THE GRANT WRITING PROCESS

The ripple effect ... magnified

Before we launch into this book proper, I want to take a moment to reassure you of your choice in picking up this knowledge-building tool. The focus is *advanced* grant writing, but it is soooo much more than that.

It is designed in such a way that it inspires action.

More than a mix of words on a page, this book offers a series of implementation steps. These are steps that, when taken, propel you from where you are today to where you want to be tomorrow. Assuming that is, that your tomorrow is a place where your business is funded and you have the additional capital you need to grow and prosper.

To help you implement what I'm sharing, I've deliberately chosen an example funding program that focuses on boosting female founders.

Why, you might ask?

Using a real-life funding program targeting women will give you real-world experience and knowledge to embed immediately into your fund-raising activities.

You will learn how to interpret the critical criteria of a grant program. By understanding this, you will be able to understand the frequent questions that would-be investors are likely to ask.

There is a mock grant application template available for you, taking inspiration from many different funding programs and grouping the most commonly asked questions.

When you understand the breakdown of a grant application,

including how to craft your responses, you will leverage this go-to operational document to curate a robust and on-point pitch deck.

Taking the time to prepare foundational support documentation that underpins your grant application – such as the growth plan, project outline, and budget allocation – will send signals to the ecosystem that you are ready.

That is why this book's ripple effect can potentially deliver more income from more opportunities than you ever previously considered.

I absolutely guarantee it.

EQUITY-FREE FUNDING

What is it? And why do you want it?

Most venture capital funding is offered to businesses in exchange for a share of ownership via a formal shareholder agreement. For example, you may offer a 10% equity stake in your business in exchange for $200,000 in venture capital.

That is equity finance.

Equity-free funding is external capital (*money*) for your business, offered without the need to exchange equity in your business (*a share of ownership*).

The most common type of equity-free funding are government, corporate or philanthropic grants. In general, grants are offered to fund projects that deliver defined outcomes. The funding is provided unencumbered (*no security is required*) under a formal contract or agreement.

Here's something I'd like you to stop and think about.

How long would it take to generate the equivalent of $100k in income via your standard sales process? And what is the cost to the business to generate that $100k in additional revenue?

If you can apply for (and receive) an additional $100k of 'free' operational capital, then why wouldn't you apply for it?

BTW … when I mention 'free,' it means there isn't a *monetary* cost to secure the cash injection. Sure, there is a cost of time and effort commitment to produce a winning funding application, but that isn't considered a cost associated with your P&L.

Another type of equity-free funding which is growing in availability and popularity is revenue-based financing. In simple terms, this is a debt-financing product offered to growing businesses and repaid over an agreed, short-term period (between two and five years). An interest rate is applied to the debt amount, and repayments are structured as a percentage of revenue. For founders, the attraction to this type of funding product is the flexibility and the ability to ramp up or scale back repayments *as required* in line with revenue fluctuations.

While it is a debt product and similar to commercial lending products offered by traditional financial institutions such as banks, funders offering bespoke financing can be more flexible in their assessment of worthy recipients of the funding ... unlike banks, which have strict lending criteria and are bound by stringent corporate governance policies.

As more revenue-based financing products become available, I encourage you to do your due diligence and engage with your accountant to seek solid financial advice about the right product and type of funder for you.

To kick off your investigation, take a look at:

- Tractor Ventures
- Affordable Loans via Community Lenders (Bank of America/Tory Burch Foundation)
- ClearCo
- Social Enterprise Finance Australia (SEFA)
- Coralus, formally SheEO

Each will have its lending criteria, but learning how to prepare a robust grant application will give you an advantage over others who haven't tried to understand the fundamentals.

As you progress through the sections and chapters that follow, you will begin to see how everything is interlinked and how to leverage one opportunity into another. It really is exciting once you start to see what is possible.

Anatomy of a Grant Program

LET'S START AT THE BEGINNING – WITH AN OVERVIEW

Grants are generally amounts of money offered by governments, charitable organisations or philanthropists and are established with very specific objectives in mind.

To help applicants understand the funding program, the program management team will prepare a detailed document called the Grant Opportunity Guideline or Program Overview. This document is the place to start when you are investigating a grant for alignment with your business and your funding need.

The Program Overview will provide a breakdown of all the critical pieces of information such as: desired program outcomes, applicant eligibility, and examples of evidence you will need to provide to secure the funding.

If you skip reading this essential document, it can make it complicated for you later when you realise a fundamental part of your application is missing.

These documents can be incredibly long and detailed, at times even confusing. I get why you might be tempted to skip it! I'm going to ask you to read it anyway – from start to finish. Yep, every single page. The time you give to this document at the beginning of your process will save you anguish in the long run.

Let's jump into reviewing a sample grant program now.

The Boosting Female Founders Initiative (BFFI)

BFFI is an Australian program offering grants between $100,000 and $480,000 to successful applicants who are majority-female-owned and led entities. The grant is awarded to startups ready to expand their businesses into domestic and global markets.

Even though this grant program is experiencing significant delays in awarding funding to applicant recipients, I've chosen it because of its focus on advancing women entrepreneurs. It is also a good example of a program focusing on commercialising innovative products.

There is a total funding pool of $52.2 million[4] to be made available over five years. The total funding pool of each funding round changes slightly from year to year. Still, an average round would be equivalent to $10.5 million and allocated to as many successful applicants as possible.

The other reason I like this funding opportunity as an example is that the minimum grant amount available is $100,000, and the maximum is $480,000. It is hard to find grants offering this level of support, so when you find one, especially for women founders, it is important to be well-positioned to throw your hat in the ring!

Before we progress any further, I invite you to download the Grant Opportunity Guidelines for the Boosting Female Founders Initiative so that you can easily follow along.

You can access it via www.funding4growth.io/book-bonuses then click on the 'download' button next to Boosting Female Founders Opportunity Guidelines.

Alternatively, you may have your own grant program that you've identified as a potential opportunity for your business. That's great too. Go to the funder or program website and download the support documents. It is a perfect time to use the information in this book to guide your application process.

---

4 All funding amounts relating to Boosting Female Founders Initiative are AUD (*Australian Dollars*)

Are you ready ...?

Now that you've got the guideline open let's kick-off.

Do you remember when I mentioned reading the guideline from start to finish? What I meant to say was to get ready to become immersed in the world of grants! I'm going to ask you to go beyond reading the guideline by encouraging you to study it actively. Post-it notes and pens at the ready. We're going in …

Let's start with some of the basics.

What triggered the establishment of this funding program?

For the Boosting Female Founders Initiative, the program became **part of the 2018 and 2020 Women's Economic Security Statements,** which were designed to help support more Australian women into work while at the same time meeting Australia's international obligations under the Convention on the Elimination of all forms of Discrimination Against Women (CEDAW).

This funding program aims to provide **targeted support** on a **co-contribution basis to female founders** of startup businesses (startups) by offering funding to help them **scale** their businesses into **domestic and global markets**.

The program is designed to provide expert mentoring and advice to meritorious applicants.

The key takeaways for you to note are:
- The program has a global view;
- It is designed to offer targeted support;
- Female founders are the key audience;
- Founders are expected to co-contribute financially;
- The funding is to support scaling a business; and
- Markets to be serviced by successful applicants are both domestic and global.

If I were an applicant looking at this funding program, before I went any further, I would be asking myself ...

Am I ready to **scale** my business nationally or internationally? If the answer was yes, then I would proceed.

If I couldn't answer yes with confidence, then I would proceed with investigating the opportunity, but I wouldn't be totally committed to the idea of applying. When I had more information available, I would decide to apply or wait for another time.

That being said, as a mentor, I am a huge supporter of anyone with the time available to progress with a draft application, because it is always an excellent learning experience. It also helps to sharpen your marketing message! More on that later.

Let's continue to break down the program further by identifying all the relevant information.

CHAPTER 1
Understanding Program Outcomes

Ready to dive into the juicy bits ...

The first thing to look for in the guideline of any funding program is the outcomes. These are the funder's objectives, that is, what they want to see happen as a result of funding being offered. It's the fundamental reason for the funding program to exist. Outcomes could be as simple as financing the installation of energy-efficient equipment, or a funder might want to support innovative projects that target vulnerable communities that seek to improve childhood development.

Whatever it may be, outcomes are always program-specific, generally well-defined, often measurable, and can vary considerably from one program to the next. It might take you a grant or two to get your head around program outcomes, but once you do, you'll begin to see a pattern. Once you've understood the pattern, you'll be able to group similar grant opportunities. When you know your *go-to* grant category or group, you can easily leverage an application completed for one opportunity into developing the next opportunity.

That is exactly how I leveraged my first $10,000 grant into $2.4 million.

Let's crack on!

Together, our focus right now is to review the program outcomes for the Boosting Female Founders Initiative (BFFI) so that you know what to expect when reviewing other programs.

BFFI has a range of program outcomes. You'll find them published in the Opportunity Guideline, but here's what to look for.

The intended outcomes of the program are:

- increased number of startups **founded** and **sustained** by women;
- **new** products and services brought to market by startups founded by women;
- **increased financial investment** in startups founded by women;
- **improved earning potential for women** through entrepreneurship;
- **facilitated mentor** relationships to support the entrepreneurial development of women; and
- increased job creation and economic growth.

Now that you understand what the defined program outcomes are, the next step is to ask yourself core eligibility questions.

- If your business were to receive the funding, how could you contribute to the achievement of one or more of the outlined goals?

What evidence can you supply that demonstrates how you've successfully contributed to the same or similar goals previously?

Going a step further ...

We already know this program has committed to providing targeted support on a **co-contribution basis to female founders of startup businesses to scale into domestic and global markets**. And ... the program will also offer expert mentoring and advice to a select number of eligible applicants.

Looking deeper into the Opportunity Guideline, you'll also find the objectives of the program are to:

- **stimulate** private sector investments into innovative startups led by women;
- help women entrepreneurs **overcome barriers to accessing finance** and support necessary to scale their startups;
- **enable female founders to scale up, expand** into domestic and/or global markets, and **become self-sufficient**; and
- **boost the economy** by increasing the diversity of startup founders.

In short, the Australian government was looking to entrepreneurs to attract more investment funding into the startup ecosystem. This is coupled with the objective of helping women become financially self-sufficient while also boosting the national economy through employing more diverse people (because diverse founders employ a more diverse workforce).

Do your business objectives align with the objectives of the BFFI funding program?

If you choose to work through this book using a funding program that you have sourced, make sure you're clear on the outcomes and objectives before looking at how your business may be a good fit.

Now that you understand what the program

management team is looking for as a return on their investment, you have a basic framework for your application.

Our next step is to understand the different ways applicant eligibility will be assessed.

CHAPTER 2
Applicant Eligibility Criteria

Not to be confused with Application Assessment Criteria

If you've applied for a grant in the past, you'll likely be aware of the distinct stages of application assessment. However, if you're new to the grant application process, here's what you need to know.

The first stage is eligibility. The second stage is an assessment of your ability to successfully deliver a funded project, i.e., meet defined program outcomes.

Applicant eligibility will immediately weed out applications from those who don't identify as the target audience for the funding. As an assessor, I review applications for assessment only from applicants that fit the target audience criteria.

It has often surprised me how many founders will choose to ignore this eligibility criteria. Over the years, I've had countless founders say to me things like, 'Once an assessor reads my application and learns about my amazing business, they will ignore the rules and give me the funding.'

If you've overheard comments like this from others, I'm sorry, but the rules are rarely ignored. The program management team will, without doubt, be accountable to a governing body responsible for ensuring all funding is allocated correctly and within the defined scope.

When reviewing the applicant eligibility criteria, it is essential to be completely honest with yourself because I can assure you that the program management team will do checks as part of a Stage 1 checkpoint. Only those applicants who meet the eligibility criteria will proceed to the application assessment phase.

You will typically find the eligibility rules in the Grant Opportunity Guidelines.

For the Boosting Female Founders Initiative (BFFI), here is a summary of the criteria you need to meet to be eligible to apply. When exploring alternative funding opportunities, be sure to look for similar criteria in the provided documentation.

You are invited to apply to BFFI if:

- Your business is an **eligible entity**;
- An **eligible project** has been scoped out; and
- The project has a breakdown of **eligible expenditures**.

What is an eligible entity? For BFFI, an eligible entity is a business incorporated in Australia, a partnership, a sole trader, or a trust/trustee.

Here's where it immediately gets tricky.

If you are a sole trader, can you confirm (with conviction) that your business is ready to scale nationally and/or internationally? Are you structured and ready for investment? Do you have a growing workforce? While a sole trader is eligible to apply, it is unlikely that a sole trader is in a strong position to secure the funding because of the additional requirements outlined in the guideline.

Key terms and definitions

Key terms and definitions can be additional causes for confusion. When reviewing the guidelines of your chosen grant program and you stumble on words that you *think* you understand the meaning of, I advise always looking for a glossary of terms. A table of definitions is usually found in the back pages of supplied guides or part of the frequently asked questions (FAQs) section.

With that in mind, let's consider a few generic definitions to align with the language used in the grant guidelines. To help you grasp the meaning of these commonly used terms, I've prepared a table of generic definitions. You'll find that glossary in the back of this book.

If you find additional definitions that commonly trip you up, you might consider starting your own glossary of terms as a living document and adding to it over time.

Now that we've covered applicant eligibility, next we'll consider timelines.

CHAPTER 3
Application Timelines

It always takes longer than you wish it would

Being realistic about timelines is super important. Program management teams and the assessors they engage will often take months to assess the applications received. All applications are given the same thoughtful consideration and must be assessed before the management team responds to you with a funding decision.

Why does it take so long?

Well, let's take Boosting Female Founders (BFFI) as a perfect example.

In 2021, there were ~2,000 applications received and the program team needed to reduce that to ~200 applications for Stage 2 of the application assessment process, which in turn is reduced to a shortlist of ~75. That shortlist is further reducedto the final group of ~30 funded applications.

Even with a large group of assessors in multiple assessment panels, it takes a lot of time.

I love that BFFI publishes its timelines, but many programs do not. That is because it is difficult to know how many initial applications will be received and, therefore the time required to determine who gets funded.

Here are the BFFI dates, as an example:

- Program Stage 1 opened in May 2022;
- Program Stage 1 closed on 2 June 2022;
- Expected Stage 2 opening in early September 2022;
- Expected Stage 2 closing in late September 2022; and
- Expected successful notifications in January 2023.

Understanding the timeline is important for three reasons:

1. Factoring the potential funding into your cash flow forecast at the right time is critical for successfully managing your operational capital;
2. Allocating an achievable project start date will be dependent on when the final notifications are distributed to successful applicants, which also has a flow-on effect on any milestones and key deliverables; and
3. Knowing how much time you have to prepare your application helps you allocate team tasks and schedule time for investigations and engagement.

I don't know about you, but I've always found it hard to keep timelines realistic. Like most entrepreneurs, I think I can do twice as much in half the time. What ultimately happens is I experience feelings of overwhelm, then burnout hits. The energy required to pull me out of a slump distracts my attention from opportunities that would genuinely benefit me and my business growth.

Taking a moment to map key dates on a timeline will help you to take stock and be ready for the time-related ups and downs that inevitably come. For example, after the huge adrenaline high of submitting your application on time comes the disappointment associated with the long wait before a decision is made about whether to fund your project. What are you going to do in the months between application submission (September 2022) and receiving a final determination (January 2023)? My advice is simple. Continue with business as usual, meaning it is critical that you return your focus to growing your business organically.

I've seen many founders submit applications for funding in May, with an expectation (and hope) that the money will be in the business account by July. It almost never happens that way.

With realistic expectations supported by good planning, you'll move through the funding experience with more joy and less disappointment, all the while continuing to grow your business and build momentum.

If you haven't already, take a moment to note the timelines associated with the grant program you're exploring.

Next, we'll begin the process of looking at the allowable activities that are eligible (or ineligible) for funding.

CHAPTER 4
Applicant Eligible Activities

Knowing what is allowable and what is not ...

This is the foundation of your application. When applying for external funding using any of the many funding products and sources available, it is important to confidently know what you intend on using the money for. I'm often surprised by entrepreneurs who stumble across a funding opportunity, see the dollars available, and promptly jump into the application form to start filling it out.

This approach is very knee-jerk and aligns with the 'wing and a prayer' method. Applying for available funding because it is available is not the most strategic of approaches. Ultimately, you're likely to a) waste your time and b) feed into an underlying belief system that you're not fundable, which is totally untrue.

Rather than leaving it to fate, I *strongly* encourage you to take a more methodical approach, starting with referring back to the Grant Opportunity Guidelines.

In the guidelines, you'll find paragraphs that specifically discuss project eligibility or eligible activities. This is where you'll see that next-level detail you'll need to understand what is included in an application with a higher probability of being funded.

Referencing back to our sample program, Boosting Female Founders (BFFI), in order to be considered, the activities you are proposing to deliver must demonstrate how your startup business intends to scale into domestic and/or global markets. Remember, it was one of the key program outcomes.

Now, what does that statement actually mean?

If we think about the meaning of the word *how* it can be described as:

In what way; or

By what means?

In grant applications, the *how* can be described by detailing the *steps* you plan to take to scale your business into domestic and/or global markets.

If you need a reminder of the definition of *scale*, refer to the table of definitions at the back of this book.

For reference, here is a breakdown of the **types of activities considered eligible** for the BFFI funding:

- Launching and scaling products or services;
- Expanding teams;
- Professional development;
- Development and marketing; and
- Expansion into other markets.

To demonstrate how to interpret these activities and how they might apply to your business, let's start with the first point – launching and scaling products or services.

You would likely read the word *launch* and believe that launch activities are considered eligible. And they are, but this is where it gets tricky. When defining your project activities, it is important to look at everything from a holistic perspective while preparing your detailed steps.

The word *launch* is often associated with being one of the first activities you *do* when launching a brand new business.

In the context of BFFI, it means a launch process that enables scale. Therefore, the assumption is that your business is already successfully operating in a market that loves what you offer, and the business is ready to rapidly expand into new markets. That rapid expansion process is often facilitated by launching into a new market.

Do you see the difference? Launching into a new market is not the same as launching into your first market.

BFFI is designed to support expansion into new markets. Therefore, all your eligible project activities must use that baseline from which you build all your steps.

Each of the other numbered points above build on this fundamental requirement. For example, expanding your team is not the same as establishing your team of first hires. Professional development specifically refers to activities that may assist you with becoming the CEO of a global company, as well as investment education and support. Development and marketing refers to the activities that support the steps you're taking to *expand* into domestic or global markets.

Understanding the distinct phases of a business when considering a Product Development Roadmap is also helpful at this time. We'll go into the Product Development Roadmap more in Chapter 15. All you need to know for now is that eligible activities are this specific.

If you're struggling to identify what your eligible activities might be and the steps to complete them, a worthwhile exercise is to look into a successfully funded business that inspires you. Understand, as much as you can around what their expansion journey has been. Knowing the steps they took and over what timeframe will help you to visualise a map of your own future. Let their success inspire your next steps.

Now for one of my favourite topics – project planning. Time to get nerdy!

CHAPTER 5
Defining the Project

So ... what is your project?

The majority of grant programs that you apply to will expect a series of activities to be delivered within a defined timeframe with proposed (but quantifiable) outcomes.

That, my friends, is a project.

Start date. End date. Activities. Outcomes. Milestones. Due dates.

Many women I've worked with will shudder at the thought of preparing a project plan. The reality is that project planning is simple *(much like a lasagne recipe)*, but it does require time and focus.

For now, start by considering your overarching project outcome or your one significant goal. Always look to the funding program guidelines for more insight. For example, in the case of BFFI:

> *A project is focused on the steps you plan to take*
> *– to launch and scale into domestic and / or*
> *global markets – within a defined timeframe.*

Sound easy? Well, kind of.

Like a recipe, your project plan is a series of steps, one building on the previous one, towards achieving that defined goal.

Using the above example, what are the steps you plan to take when launching into a global market? If you're a little lost on where to start, I encourage you to take a moment to think back to your initial launch activities when you started your business. What actions did you take to get your business in front of your key target audience? What outcomes were achieved from those actions?

If you're already planning to scale your business, maybe you've already engaged the services of a market development agency or a commercialisation consultant. If so, I expect they have prepared a list of actions for you as part of a growth plan. Simply cut and paste those actions and drop them into your funding application.

We'll talk about your team in the Management Capability (Chapter 8), but this is one of the obvious benefits of engaging the right people with the right skills and experience at the right time.

When your project is BAU

You may already be familiar with the acronym BAU, it stands for 'business as usual.' Funders have a complete aversion to anything in your project plan that resembles BAU activities. Why? Funders want to see that you've considered the series of activities required to achieve your growth goals as they relate to their program objectives.

They want to be able to de-risk the allocation of funding to ensure the applicants who are funded are low risk to successfully deliver what they promise. The project plan, because of the level of detail included in it, helps assessors to determine the risk level associated with an application.

For example, the following activities are immediate *red flags* to assessors and their concern is reflected in the assessment score.

There is a lack of detail in the project plan;

Activities or steps are too high-level and not specific enough;

Market demand is not obvious, and validation activities are missing from the plan;

Forecasted growth goals are too low and not reflective of a scaling business model; and

The market launch reads like standard day-to-day operations.

Early-stage businesses with micro-teams are desperate for any funding they can secure to help meet day-to-day financial needs. Activities focusing on customer account management are basic daily actions required to support existing customers of your product. While critical to the long-term sustainable success of your business, they are not considered a valid *project activity*.

Remember that a project has a start date and an end date. Project-related activities will only be performed between those dates and generally not at any other time. For example, if you're organising a bespoke marketing event specifically for your prospective *new* international audience, then it becomes a project activity. If the marketing event is for your existing customer base, then it is considered BAU.

As you develop your project plan, consistently ask yourself if the activity is project-related or BAU. This will help you to make a conscious distinction between the two. I recommend crafting a list of all the obvious BAU activities

currently performed in your business today, then refer back to that list as you prepare your project plan. It will help to clarify project versus BAU activity.

Next, let's talk budget.

CHAPTER 6

Budget and Deliverables

Delving into the detail

Following on from the previous chapter, where we started the conversation about the project to be funded, next we build on the list of fundable activities to create a full delivery plan. Plus, we align activities and timelines to a budget.

In the project delivery plan, you began breaking down your planned activities step by step. Now, you assign a cost against each one.

Taking the Boosting Female Founders (BFFI) example, you've likely begun to rely on the detailed information provided in the document to help clarify what is fundable and what is not. It is important to note that not all program management teams are as thorough as the BFFI team. Suppose you're referring to a program guide that is lacking in detail around allowable project activities. In that case, I encourage you to go all Sherlock Holmes and dive deep into the section that explains the budget and what can be included.

You may find additional financial or budget-related information pertaining to eligible expenditure items in the appendix of the program guidelines, in the program FAQs, or as downloadable attachments on the grant program webpage.

Clearly understanding what can be included in the funding budget and what can't will give you direction and reassurance on what activities can be undertaken. Whenever I work backward from the budget to determine what actions to take, I call this process *reverse-engineering project deliverables*.

Eligible expenditure

It doesn't matter from which funding program you are seeking funding; there will be a standard approach applied. For an expenditure item to be eligible and on the approved list, it must:

- Be a direct cost of the project;
- Be incurred by your business to deliver the outlined project; and
- Be spent within the project timeline.

The timing of these expenses is critical. For example, the business must incur all project expenditures after the project start date and be spent before the defined end date in order for it to be eligible.

In some cases, with permission from the funding program team, founders can choose to commence their projects from the date they are notified that their application has been successful. These deviations from the standard process are given *on occasion* when there are lengthy delays anticipated with contract execution, especially if a minister of government is required for signing.

Importantly, you must *confirm* that this is allowable. Otherwise, you risk paying out project-related expenses that will not be covered by grant funding. This is why dates are crucial.

Contractually binding expenditure

If you're new to applying for grants of $100,000 or more, you may not be aware of the need to enter into binding contracts with funders. When funders are offering larger sums of money, they want to be confident that you're going to deliver what you say you're going to deliver and spend money only on the things you've outlined in your budget.

Contracts help funders hold fundees accountable more easily. If you thought you could wing it and make it up as you go, you may want to consider the legal ramifications of that approach. The majority (if not all) of the contracts I've seen include clauses that allow funders to seek compensation if fundees don't deliver in line with agreed expectations.

Yes, that means they will ask for the supplied funds to be returned. Nobody wants that.

The underlying message here is this:

- Know what activities can be included in your project delivery plan;
- Clearly assign a calculated budget item against each of those deliverables; and
- Don't make it up!

If your application for funding is successful, the program manager may ask you to verify the project costs provided in the application by supplying preliminary quotes for the proposed work. Additionally, at the time of project acquittal, the program team may ask you to provide evidence of expenditure, such as paid invoices for major costs, copies of bank statements showing project-related outgoings, or an audited copy of your project-related financial statements.

Remember, when funders are offering funding, they are accountable for the monies issued. This means there is a layer of governance to ensure everything is above board.

Project variations

This seems like a suitable time to discuss project variations because every project plan I've developed has used a series of underlying assumptions to drive the development of desired project outcomes. Often, when a project has kicked off, and engagement with key stakeholders is underway, assumptions are either proven to be correct or they need to be adjusted.

In simple terms, the activities that I thought would deliver predefined outcomes are not achieving the desired result, and therefore, I need to pivot.

The first time this happened to one of my funded projects, I panicked for weeks! *What is the impact on the contract (or funding agreement) I signed? Will I need to repay the total in funding that was already paid to me? Will I be blacklisted from ever being given a grant again?*

In my true maverick style, I immediately looked for loops I could exploit and angles I could pitch. I was 100% pure hustle persona. My panic created chaos until one day, I thought, *fuck it*. I just need to call my assigned program manager and tell them what I am struggling with. I need to be honest.

My inexperienced self was blown away by how understanding the team was about my predicament. They knew more about these situations than I did, and I found them to be incredibly helpful and insightful. I was so relieved to learn that I could simply apply for a project variation, and there was no need for my maverick self to make an appearance.

What is a project variation exactly? It is a document where you detail how the project is deviating from the original intention. What activities are changing? Is there a change to the budget? Are you still tracking to deliver the agreed outcomes? Depending on how far the project is moving away from what was originally planned, you may be asked to complete a new project delivery plan and budget. At the very least, you'll be asked to put the variation in writing as an addendum to the original contract or agreement.

A word of caution, if you need to submit a project variation, be sure that you're diligent with your assigned budget items because it is unlikely that you'll be given additional funds.

Record-keeping

If your application is successful, you may be asked to verify the project budget that you provided in your application. This will mean supplying evidence, such as quotes for major costs.

Payment records of all eligible expenditures are expected during project progress reporting and for final grant acquittal. If records are not provided when requested, the expense may not qualify as eligible expenditure, and means you may be asked to repay amounts of funding provided to you. Do not leave yourself open to this type of risk! Always plan to keep thorough financial records throughout the whole project.

At the end of the funded project, an independent financial audit of all eligible expenditures from the project may be required. Some funders will allow an audit expense to be included in the project budget. Carefully check the guidelines for confirmation, and always email the program manager if you need assistance.

When preparing your budget, take particular care to understand what is considered an eligible expense and what is not. Knowing what to avoid from the outset is the best course of action. That way, you don't waste time planning and costing activities that will immediately render your application invalid. We'll go into more detail in Chapter 19.

But, for now, our focus will shift to evidence.

CHAPTER 7
Evidence and Support

Evidence ... what evidence?

Some grant applications will make their requirement for evidence very explicit. For example, you may be asked to upload support documentation or letters from current or prospective customers.

Here's the thing. Not all support documents are created equal.

Uploading random 'story-telling' documents – unless specifically asked for – may do more damage than you expect. **Assessors are looking for support documents that validate claims you've made in your application responses.**

If you've mentioned the names of some well-known brands on board as testers or financial customers of your product, then a letter of support from them is powerful.

A word of warning when it comes to letters of support, though. Do *not* prepare canned responses or templated letters for your supporters. Letters must be prepared by genuine advocates of your business, and they must articulate their specific problem and how your product provides a solution.

If your letters of support are from strategic partners, it will be expected that they will articulate the problem experienced by *their* customers or members along with outlining why a partnership with you and your business aligns with their strategic objectives in providing a solution to the known customer problem. They would also outline what their contribution is to the partnership and to your proposed funded project.

Customer reviews

What about reviews or testimonials from existing customers?

These can be helpful but should not be your primary evidence. They are good complementary pieces when they speak to specific, defined features of your product. They may even touch on project outcomes. But here's the trap. If you have too many testimonials from customers or users of your product, then the assessors will question if your product is already fully commercialised in the market.

Stay with me ...

Using BFFI as our example, key program outcomes include:

- New products and services brought to the market by women-owned businesses;
- For women to increase their earning potential through entrepreneurship; and
- To scale up into domestic or international markets.

If your testimonials confirm that you have raving fans of your product in your existing market segment and your project objective is to scale into a *new international market*, those previous reviews demonstrate a level of market-to-product fit that can be leveraged into the new market segment.

This means you've already got a successful marketing message in a market that results in sales. *Woohoo!* You also have a distribution model and channel that works. *Double woohoo!!*

The assumptions that underpin your funding application might be to:

- Test existing marketing messaging in the new market;
- Adapt the existing marketing messaging for new users;
- Test existing distribution model in the new market;
- Adapt the existing distribution model for new users; or
- Partner with collaborators to open access to new users.

Previous testimonials are helpful, but they are not the end-game. Use them to build confidence and to help demonstrate a strong starting point. By themselves, they may not be reflective of your ultimate goal.

Submitting evidence

As I've implied briefly, some of the more complex funding programs, like BFFI, will split the application process into two stages or phases. Stage 1 is often an expression of interest (EOI). Stage 2 is when a more comprehensive application is prepared. It is usually during Stage 2 that your support documentation is requested. For example, in BFFI Stage 2, you must also provide:

- Evidence to support your source of funding (e.g., a letter from project contributors confirming their funding amount);
- A pitch deck presented in PDF or PowerPoint (maximum ten slides) and/or link to a video pitch from your CEO (maximum five minutes) supporting your response to the assessment criteria;
- A business plan, including revenue model, customer acquisition and company management structure, project scope, delivery methodology, timeframes, budget, risks, and how you will measure the success of the project; and
- A trust deed (where applicable).

Other types of evidence requested may also relate to validating your eligibility or claims.

If you are working through your own funding program, start a list of requested supporting documentation, i.e., evidence. You'll find more information about what is required in the program guidelines or FAQs.

Speaking of evidence and demonstrating capability, the next chapter focuses on management capability and things to remember.

CHAPTER 8
Management Capability

The subjectivity of capability

The Oxford Dictionary tells us that *capability* is the power or ability to do something[5].

Through the assessment process, assessors are seeking to determine the extent to which applicants can deliver what they say they're going to deliver. They will look for key information in your application and compare it against the objectives of the grant program and the outcomes they're seeking. For example, when scaling a business – growing your business at a rapid pace – there is an expectation that your business is more than just you. There must be a team surrounding you, helping you to grow and expand. Not just any team. Assessors are looking for indicators that applicants have *the right team* engaged.

So, when preparing your response to a question that asks about management capability, it is important to consider your management team. Specifically, your *project* management team.

Remember, the **overarching goal of your project is to launch and scale into domestic and global markets**.

---

5 Source Oxford Dictionary via Google search

While your project outline will be focused on all the steps required to achieve the above overarching goal, the budget aligns with the project delivery plan, and the project team will demonstrate delivery capability. See how everything starts to fit neatly into each other? One block building upon the other.

A recommendation for your consideration … If your goal is to scale, be sure to have people on your delivery team who have real-world experience in successfully scaling a business (similar to yours) into a market (similar to or the same as the market you're aspiring to enter). This is your opportunity to sing the praises of your team and showcase each person with the skills and experience in delivering high-value projects.

When preparing to showcase your team, consider how you may best highlight their expertise by sharing success stories and detailing their track record. Emphasising problem-solving skills and high levels of adaptability and flexibility will build confidence in your application, especially if references and reviews align with previous key performance indicators (KPIs) and success metrics.

Have you ever stopped to think about what team mix will instil confidence? You may or may not know that angel and venture capital investors use formulas when making their investment decisions. One of the common go-tos is a formula around team. For an investor to feel confident in the ability of your team, they look for certain roles: CEO – likely to be you; a range of *chiefs* – as in Chief Technology Officer, Chief Financial Officer, Chief Operations Officer; then come the *heads-of* – Head of Marketing, Head of People and Culture, Head of Sales, Head of Customer Experience and Support; throw in a Product Manager and a Legal and Compliance Adviser, and that's your tier one, sure-to-be-funded team.

Sure, the focus of this book is advanced *grant* writing, not venture capital investment, but many grant funders and their management teams look to the investment ecosystem for inspiration and guidance. If an investor formula breaks down a fundable team as being full of chiefs and heads-of, then high-value grant programs will often do the same.

It is, however, important to be realistic about building your team. If you don't have a pipeline of sales to justify spending the operational capital on big salaries, that's okay. Instead, look for ways to innovate and adapt. Consider recruiting an advisory panel of semi-retired chiefs or heads-of and bolster your everyday operational team that way.

If you don't already have a Sara Blakely (American businesswoman and philanthropist) equivalent within your salaried staff or on your co-founding team, then look to external advisers, mentors or panels. And if you do, *lucky you!*

Consider the value that experienced investors can contribute to your business. Have you noticed on television shows like *Dragon's Den* or *Shark Tank* – when multiple investors are pitching themselves to the founder – that they often pitch their previous success and achievements as additional value-adds to the business? This strategy can be incredibly fruitful for both the investor, who gets a return sooner, and the founder, who gets to grow their business faster.

Funders are also becoming more proactive in recognising they must contribute more than just dollars. That is why government agencies and corporations are beginning to offer supplementary programs that harness the vast depth of skills and experience residing in internal teams. Through specialist knowledge, coupled with the mighty power of the government or corporate procurement systems, funding programs are offering immersive validation opportunities along with partnership introductions for users. Innovative funders are increasingly savvy in understanding that they too have an obligation to contribute to a grant recipient's sustainable success.

Do you have your dream team in place, or are they yet to materialise? Documenting the skills, experience and culture you want as your business grows will simultaneously help you ground your vision into reality and support your bid to secure funding.

When researching funding opportunities for your business, also consider the value of tapping into external specialist teams. They may not be with you long-term, but their impact will.

ANATOMY OF A GRANT PROGRAM RECAP

Pause and take a breath

If you're still with me, *thank you,* and congratulations!

It is a big jump from small $5,000 or $10,000 grants into categories offering $100,000 or more.

You're possibly asking yourself: *WTF?*

And: *Is it worth it?*

My response will always be: *Absolutely, yes!*

So many nuggets of gold are hidden in the process of applying for large-scale grants. You will always apply what you learn to other areas of your business. Examples include refining the strategic growth plan, calculating operational budgets, and reassessing the skills within your team. Every component of a grant application adds value to your business. I promise!

Let's take stock

Now that you've worked your way through the example

grant program, you'll have a better understanding of why the funder is making the funding available and a high-level appreciation for the key elements considered when preparing your application to be funded.

It is also a good time to take a moment to set realistic expectations. What do I mean by that?

Well ...There is always a finite pot of money available when funding rounds open for applications. For Round 3 of Boosting Female Founders a total of $11.6 million was offered.

To get a sense of how many applications will be funded, we can use the following assumptions:

- Assumption #1 – The majority of successful applicants will request the maximum amount of funding available.
- Assumption #2 – The ratio split between what is considered a Priority Group and Non-Priority Group will be 60:40 (note – this is my unconfirmed assumption).

So ...

	Total Value of Pool	Ratio Successful Applications	Max. Value of Grant	No. of Successful Applications
Priority Group	$6,960,000	60%	$480,000	15
Non-Priority Group	$4,640,000	40%	$400,000	12
	$11,600,000			26

As a founder of a business keen for additional funding to support business growth, $11,600,000 sounds like a *helluva* lot of money, and it is. Yet, when you break it down to calculate how many successful applications will be funded, a different story emerges.

Based on my assumptions and calculations above, there will be

~26 applications funded. This is a program that received ~2,000 applications in 2021. To be one of the lucky 26 successful applicants, your application needs to be strong enough to be considered in the top ~1.5% of all applications received.

Let that figure sink in for a moment.

Your immediate response is probably: *Why TF would I bother?* I'm with you. I know how you're feeling. I've felt like that too. But I'm here to tell you that it is certainly possible.

If I can, you can too ...

I can remember being successful in receiving a small $10,000 grant and then looking at an opportunity to secure $80,000. The doubting voice that sits inside your mind was also active inside mine, but I took the steps outlined in the previous chapters to properly understand the opportunity. I downloaded the Grant Opportunity Guidelines, and I read that document from cover to cover, page by page, and line by line.

Armed with a clear understanding of the opportunity, I took steps to secure a collaborative partnership that delivered the strengths I was lacking in my team capability. That partnership added so much value to my project. We successfully secured the $80,000 and then levelled up to secure $860,000 when the next grant opportunity presented itself.

Seriously, if I can do it, you can too.

In the next section, our focus will be on the application itself. We will use a sample application form that I've created, and we will break it down section by section to help you understand precisely what is being requested and why.

While I have been using and will continue to reference the Boosting

Female Founders Initiative as a guide, the application template we are using is *not* the application from BFFI. The sample application is a mix of different programs and applications I've previously worked on as an assessor, or I've seen in my time as an applicant.

I encourage you to download the application template via www.funding4growth.io/book-bonuses and then use the next section as an activity-based learning opportunity.

By completing the application as you progress through the next section, you will learn so much more than reading the words on a page.

If you're ready … let's jump into it now!

SECTION 2

Getting Started

Preparation is key to securing funding

Are you ready to dive into the deep end? Hopefully, you've answered with a *hell yes!* Not only are you ready to build your draft $100,000 application, but you're so keen you're dancing in your chair.

Before we jump into the *doing* of the application, let's take a moment to remember the purpose of an application.

Funders have a pool of funds. They really want to allocate it. Not some of it. All of it. Why? The team who pitched the funding program to decision-makers has already contributed a significant amount of time and money to:

- Define the problem(s) to be solved;
- Justify why that specific pool of funding is needed; and
- Demonstrate how specialists in their field (*you*) can deliver solutions.

Funding program designers genuinely believe that smart, innovative entrepreneurs hold the key in resolving problems that negatively impact the world we live in. These might be societal, environmental, or technological. Whatever the driver, the program team are committed to catalysing change for good with the funds they have.

It is important to reiterate that even though funders want to allocate 100% of the funds available in their funding pool, they must do so responsibly. Every single dollar of funding must be accounted for, not only to the senior management team but also to the team that provides financial and audit oversight.

To demonstrate how accountable the program team is when allocating the funding, there must be a system of traceability. The application form is one element that feeds the traceability system.

What is it about the application?

Along with asking key questions and capturing applicant responses, the application also includes a legal declaration including fundamental requirements such as:

- Adhering to privacy, confidentiality and disclosure provisions;
- Endorsing the application, program of works and project expenditure; and
- Not providing misleading or false information.

By preparing and submitting a funding application, you are formally declaring agreement to the terms and conditions of the program. Therefore, it is vital you are aware of what you're agreeing to.

In addition to the legal side of things, it is important to understand other ways in which applications are used by program teams.

Importantly, applications are the basis of assessment to award funding and the information included in the application is used to determine how suitable you and your business are to receive funding.

The method of assessing applications is complex but important to understand, which is why this topic has its own section later in Section 3 this book. For now, here is a high-level overview of the assessment process, so you have some context.

Assessment starts with:

- Are you eligible to apply?
- What do you bring to the table?
- Can you deliver what you say you're going to deliver?
- How are you going to deliver?
- What are the key benefits?

The application must contain enough detail to answer assessor questions, while also being inspiring. Think Brené Brown and her book *Daring Greatly*[6]. As a research professor at the University of Houston, Brown's work is very structured and outcomes-based, but when she writes for a wider audience, she infuses relatable story-telling into her books to take you on a journey. Knowing her readers as well as she does, the sometimes heavy, more technical elements are woven into meaningful everyday applications.

Let me show you how.

---

6 Brown, Brené. Daring Greatly: How the Courage to be Vulnerable Transforms the Way We Live, Love, Parent and Lead. Penguin Life, 2015

CHAPTER 9
Applicant Details

Getting the basics right

If you haven't already done this, now is the time to download the draft application template from the www.funding4growth.io/book-bonuses page.

As explained previously, I've designed this application template to align with programs offering $100,000 or more, which means we will be working through an application that is more complex than if you were applying for a small scale grant of $5,000 or $10,000. The template also aligns with the type of application that you might complete when applying for a commercialisation, business incentive or growth grant.

When allocating time to complete a high-value application like this, you might spend upwards of 100 hours preparing your submission. Yup. I'm not kidding. This is a time-intensive process. But don't worry. The intention of this book is to help you develop a generic baseline application that you can use as a reference document time and time again.

Once you've got your baseline prepared, you'll find it quicker and easier to prepare applications that follow because:

- You'll know what is expected of your submission;
- You'll have done it once, so every time thereafter will be easier; and
- You'll have a resource bank from which to draw inspiration and information.

So ... shall we start?

Details, details, details

In this chapter, our focus is on completing the Applicant Details section of the application.

It is the section of the application where you fill in your business name, address, and contact details of the key contact person, along with your business identifier number[7]. You'll also outline your business structure and often your tax category.

When I'm completing an online grant application via a portal, I find it quicker and easier to have my working copy of the application open, *generally as a Google Doc,* with my key details already typed out. That way, I can simply copy and paste my responses into the correct response box in the portal; I do it this way because don't want to risk messing up something as simple as my business identifier or my email address.

It's amazing how weird and wonderful the typos get when rushing to complete an application. For that next layer of support, I also have digital tools like a business identifier online search tool[8] open to triple check I have my fundamental details correct.

Some online application forms will include validation fields.

---

7 In Australia, the business identifier number is the Australian Business Number or ABN. You will likely have the equivalent of an ABN in your country.

8 In Australia, this is called the ABN LookUp tool.

These validation checks automatically link to an online tool in the backend, with a data feed from a third party, to verify the information you've inputted. For example, address fields may prefill with a response supplied by the data provider. If so, you'll be asked to review the data to confirm or reject the address offered. The business identifier field is another that can have an automated validation on it. Some online applications will auto-populate multiple fields, including your company structure, your goods and services tax status and your registered charity status (if applicable).

All in all, this section is straightforward and by far the easiest of the whole application. Your responsibility is to complete your own checks to make sure that the fundamental information is true and correct.

Advanced Grant Writing Action
In the application template, input your fundamental information contained in the table labelled – Applicant Organisation – including fields such as your business name, identifier and address.

Done? Let's move to the next focus area, which is eligibility.

CHAPTER 10
Applicant Eligibility

Is your business eligible for this grant?

Generally, the next featured section of the application will ask you a range of questions to determine your business's eligibility to apply for the funding being offered. These questions might be short answer questions with predefined responses or a range of statements where you tick the most accurate description.

You will likely find general eligibility questions among questions asking for your business details, as outlined in the previous chapter.

Eligibility questions might be:

- Are you a sole trader, partnership or incorporated company?
- Are you a not-for-profit organisation?
- Are you a trust or a trustee?

Our sample funding program, the Boosting Female Founders Initiative (BFFI) included eligibility questions like these:

- Do women own at least 51% of your startup?
- Does the business have a combined annual turnover of less than $20 million for each of the three financial years prior to the lodgement of this application?

- Does the business have an Australian Business Number?

A word of warning! As an assessor, I've seen many applications where the applicant was careless responding to these questions, and ultimately provided incorrect responses. While this may not seem like a big deal, the funding program will have rules around who is eligible to apply and who is not. If you inadvertently tick the wrong box, you could immediately render your application ineligible.

You might be surprised to learn that assessors need to review the eligibility responses and will often perform their own checks. For example, if I'm assessing an application that is submitted by a person who appears to identify as a man and they've checked the box suggesting the business is female-led, then I will check the website and LinkedIn looking for evidence of women in leadership roles. Some applicants will tick any box they think will get them a better result.

While I can appreciate the determination of an applicant in their bid to make it through to the next stage of assessment, it is important to remind you that assessors are tasked with reducing large numbers of applications down to a shortlist. These shortlists might be as low as 10%[9] of the total applications received. I really want you to make it to the shortlist! To do so, you need to be confident that you are an eligible candidate for the funding.

Some programs, like BFFI, will take eligibility a step further by asking applicants to provide evidence. For example, applicants are required also to submit:

- A signed declaration using a provided template; and
- Certifications that the business/startup is women-owned and women-led.

Not every program is that strict, but it is important to be aware that

---

9 This is an example percentage and should be considered an arbitrary indicator only.

some are. Therefore, take your time. Read every question. Answer honestly and correctly.

Advanced Grant Writing Action
In the application template, you'll find key eligibility questions to review. Progressively work your way through them, capturing your responses in the areas provided.

If you've already identified a program that you're keen to apply to, then I encourage you to take a moment to prepare a breakdown of the eligibility criteria associated with the grant application. By taking the time to do this, you give yourself the ability to focus on exactly what is needed.

I will often use digital tools to help me break down the structure of the grant program and the application I'm preparing. One of the tools I have found really useful is Trello because it helps me see the whole picture visually rather than in a linear way on the application form. It is free to access and flexible enough to be helpful. As we work through the application, I'll give you pointers on how to use a digital tool like Trello to plan out your responses.

Now that you've completed the eligibility-related questions, it's time to get your teeth into crafting responses.

CHAPTER 11

Business Description

It's time to shine ...

The questions that ask you to describe your business in more detail will likely be the first requiring long-form responses. Before now, you may have ticked a few boxes and provided one- or two-word answers, nothing too strenuous. From this point in the application, you'll enjoy getting your creative juices flowing.

One key pointer before we drop into the activity for this chapter is to take note of the word limit assigned to each question requiring a long-form response. As you explore more grant opportunities and therefore consider more applications, you'll begin to see word limits are commonplace. These limits often range from 50 to 200 words. For research-based grant programs I have seen, on occasion, responses with limits of up to 500 words.

When completing an online application, word limits will be automatically enforced with the technology preventing you from typing more than the assigned limit. When it comes time to cut and paste your responses from your draft document into the online form, you can inadvertently lose key information if your word count exceeds what is allowable. I encourage you to be mindful and aware of these word limits as you are preparing your draft application responses.

Provide a brief overview of the applicant organisation.

Before rushing in with your first thoughts, take a moment to digest what is actually being asked by this question.

Breaking down the words within the request:

- *Brief* – Okay, got that covered with the 100-word limit;
- *Overview* – General review or summary; and
- *Applicant organisation* – Your business.

The trickiest element by far is *the overview*. What do you think an assessor wants to know to help set the scene for the remainder of the application?

- What is your product/service? – Yup, that's obvious;
- Who is your primary consumer? – Sure, this, too, is obvious;
- What is the business model? – Okay, I might not have thought about this one;

And ...

- Notable success already achieved – Really? Heck yes!

Your 100-word business description is more than your elevator pitch. It is your first opportunity to build trust and position the application as one filled with achievements that align with funding program objectives.

For example, here is a sample program objective:

The Funder will provide funding for projects that aim to develop, strengthen and grow the social enterprise ecosystem, particularly in regional communities.

So, in your 100-word description, it is sensible to *mention your achievements* in **developing, strengthening, or growing a social enterprise ecosystem**, along with a short sentence that focuses on what your future goals and objectives are.

Advanced Grant Writing Action

This is your time to shine by putting your best foot forward. Prepare your first long-form response in the application template.

While the objective of this section is to complete a first draft, let us remember to set realistic goals and expectations. As with all written submissions, you will likely prepare your first draft, which will evolve into your second, third, fourth and ultimately final draft. However, you need to start somewhere ... and your somewhere is today.

Once you're done with your *rough-draft* response, press on to the next chapter. Let's keep the momentum going.

CHAPTER 12
Product Being Commercialised

Deep dive into your product

Before we go any further, a quick reflection on terminology. Remember, you'll find a full table of definitions at the back of this book, but the one that is really important to understand right now is … **product**.

If you searched this online, you will find a range of definitions that define what a Product is. The following definition is my adaption:

Almost anything a business sells — whether physical or virtual — qualifies as a product. It is important to remember that products represent the entire experience that customers share with your company, not just the item or service itself.

What I like about this explanation is that it mentions the importance of the **customer experience**.

I've seen many a founder get stuck on terminology by asking themselves: *Am I selling a product or a service?* In the eyes of your customers, if there is a monetary exchange, then they are purchasing a product of your business - albeit perhaps a service you are delivering.

What does that mean for your grant application? Whenever you see a question asking for information about the product offered, then consider the request to include any service-based products as well.

Referencing the application template

There is usually at least one question that will ask you about the product being offered. Some applications, like the application template I've prepared for you, will have multiple product-related questions.

As a rule of thumb, *questions asking about your product are never just asking about your product*.

See the following examples from the application template that reference your product:

Question 1.3: What is the *product* you are commercialising?

Question 1.1: Provide a brief history of the development of your *product* including the amount of time it has taken to reach this point.

Question 1.5: Explain what is innovative, unique, and new about your *product* compared to what is currently in the market.

Question 1.4: Describe the significant issue, the opportunity, and the market need that your *product* will address.

Let's dig deeper.

Question 1.3 is asking about the product itself, so this one is easy enough. However, it is also important to understand the intention of the word *commercialisation*.

Commercialisation, in its basic form is taking a *new* product to the market. Commercialisation includes how you intend to produce, distribute, market, sell and provide support to the consumers of your product. It is the process of exchanging your product with a market of customers for a profitable financial return.

Therefore, when preparing your response, it is critical you touch on the complete commercialisation journey of your product.

In contrast , **Question 1.1** is asking for a brief *history* of your product development journey, communicated using a timeline. It is up to you to determine what tells the stronger story, starting from the present and working backward or starting in the past and moving forward. Either way, clearly demonstrating how the product has evolved, within a defined period of time, is the best way to prepare your response.

Question 1.5 introduces the word *innovation*. We'll cover innovation in more depth in the following chapter, but for now, consider what is new, different, or unique about your product when compared to other similar products in the market. Be clear about your product uniqueness and its secret advantage that sets it apart from others.

Question 1.4 is asking you to explain the problem being experienced by your core consumer group. If you can speak to this question from a position of lived experience, then it will be obvious in your response.

A word of warning, though … don't get carried away sharing your personal story. Touch on it, but don't lose your focus. Remember the objective of the question is for you to demonstrate that you understand the market need so well that your ability to commercialise the product is unquestionable.

If you don't have lived experience of the problem, then you will need to clearly demonstrate how you've acquired the knowledge you need to effectively engage and service your target consumer group. This could be in the form of key partnerships or collaborations, or with embedded expertise on your team. There is no right or wrong way to demonstrate your knowledge, just be sure that you do!

CHAPTER 13
Your Audience Within the Market

Everything revolves around your customer

One of the reasons women and minority groups launch businesses is because they see a real gap in the market. These gaps are evident to them because women and minority groups are often the ones impacted by an unresolved issue. These types of business owners have empathy and first-hand experience.

Be mindful when it comes to answering questions about your market, your audience, or your customer, that responses need to be less about you and more about the users of your product.

Referencing some of the questions in the application template, you'll find the following themes captured:

- How do your customers currently attempt to fill the gap they are experiencing?
- What is the market you are targeting and why this market?
- What research have you done? Include your findings and market statistics.

These questions are incredibly important because your responses will demonstrate how well you know your audience and the market and how well-planned you are for scale and growth.

If you've been through an incubator or accelerator program, you will have heard the term **product–market fit**, or sometimes reversed as **market–product–fit**.

This terminology mean that you've conducted research, engaged with your audience and listened to what they've told you they want. Then, you have purposely and consistently evolved the product to align with their need. In essence, the product fits beautifully with market need.

More on word limits

You'll notice that responses to market-related questions have 200-word limits. This is twice as many as the first section of the application; therefore, there is an expectation that assessors are looking for *more detailed* responses.

Even though more detail is assumed, it is still important to remain focused on the program outcomes and not to get lost in the story. Accurate responses that are direct and to-the-point are always best. Do not include puff and padding in your responses. Assessors see through that in an instant (personally, I find it annoying)!

Back to the application template

It doesn't matter to which grant program you're applying; there will always be at least one question in the application asking for information about your market.

Let's deep dive into some related questions in the template.

Question 2.2: Is the product you are seeking funding for currently in the market and being used by customers?

Question 2.1: Explain how the market (your potential customers) currently attempts to address the problem gap outlined in Q1.4.

Question 2.2b: Provide details of the target market and why you are targeting this market.

Question 2.3: Outline the research and analysis that has been undertaken to identify the target market(s), including key findings and any relevant market statistics.

Here are some clues for addressing these questions.

Question 2.2 wants to know if your product is already in the market and being used by paying customers. It seems like a very straightforward question, but it might not be! It may actually be used to determine your eligibility for the funding.

When innocuous questions like this one are included, I recommend referring back to the overarching objectives of the funding program. Is your business eligible for the funding if your product is already in the market and with paying customers? Some programs will definitely want your product to be successfully in the market; however, programs like BFFI want you to be in the early stages of market adoption, but not so far along that your business is no longer considered a *startup*.

Once you have clarity, then begin to craft your response by positioning your business against desired program outcomes.

See how **Question 2.1** wants you to build on a response provided in an earlier section of the application. This is a perfect example of what assessors are looking for when it comes to sharing intimate knowledge of your proposed market.

What am I talking about here? Well, it is the journey of understanding between you and your product end-user. Question 1.4 asked about your understanding of the problem being experienced, then Question 2.1 is giving you an opportunity to build on that demonstrated knowledge by explaining your understanding of how *your potential* customers are currently solving the problem they have.

My advice is to look for a series of questions in applications that help you to craft the following building blocks of knowledge – what is the problem, who is experiencing it, what is the solution, and what is the impact of you providing the solution?

Speaking of building blocks, **Question 2.2b** will build on your responses provided in 1.4, 2.1 and 2.2. This is your opportunity to explain clearly and concisely who your target audience is and why they mean so much to you. Here, you can be emotionally factual. Assessors will welcome the humanity of your response.

Finally, **Question 2.3** covers research findings.

I've seen so many founders trip up here. They arrive at this question and stare at it blankly. Or they start that unhelpful, deathly spiral of doom, thinking they've already failed because they haven't done any formal research.

The question sounds scary, but when you break it down, I promise it really isn't.

Outline the research …

… and analysis …

… to identify the target market(s) …

… including key findings …

… and any relevant market statistics.

What is research? It can be as simple as running a poll on social media or as formal as coordinating one-on-one interviews with a sample group of people. Ultimately, your research will be a process of acquiring understanding from your audience. Whatever activities you decide to perform are okay, as long as they help to inform you about your likely customer.

What is analysis? It is the process of inspecting the data collected from research activities. Raw data by itself often doesn't tell the complete story. It is only after a process of manipulation and analysis that the hidden nuggets of gold become visible.

What is a target market? That one is easy and doesn't really need explanation, but for completeness … your target market is the people who will *likely buy* your product, grouped together using a series of criteria for easy categorisation. You want to *target* that grouped audience with a shared message that resonates – and expect that they will make a purchase.

What are the key findings? After inspecting your collection of responses, you document insights about your audience. Generally, these insights result from a series of assumptions you make about who your audience is and why they want what you're offering.

What are market statistics? This includes any research activity that you've conducted and is directly related to your would-be customers. Using the insights gathered from those direct activities, you can extrapolate wider meaning by looking at overarching market statistics.

For example, here are the market statistics for housing occupancy and costs[10] in Australia. In 2020, 66% of Australian households owned their own home with or without a mortgage, and 31% of households rented their home. Average weekly housing costs were: $493 for owners with a mortgage, $54 for owners without a mortgage, $379 for renters.

Using the example as inspiration, can *you* demonstrate any correlation between your research findings and those published by

10 Source: Australian Bureau of Statistics, Survey of Housing and Income, reference period 2019-2020. Published May, 2022.

larger entities, such as government agencies? My recommendation is to always look for and include reputable references that help give credibility to your response.

One last comment about research … *please, please, please* … get into the habit of documenting all your research activities. Even if it is something as simple as researching on Google or looking for articles or reports published by others. Implementing a process of capturing information, analysing it, and drawing conclusions against your findings will save you time *and anguish* when it comes time to prepare your funding application.

I know I've used a lot of real estate on that last question, but that shows how important it is. Now, over to you.

Advanced Grant Writing Action

Commence the market-related questions in your application template but stop when you reach Question 2.4 because the next chapter on market potential will help you to complete the questions relating to the market.

If you're using a digital tool to help with organising and structure, I recommend you use it now. For example, use your Trello board to plan out responses, then add bullet points or thought provokers directly into your application template as they immediately come to mind.

You will always go back over what you've dropped into the template so spend the time you need to craft your responses properly.

CHAPTER 14
Market Potential

Exploring your audience as a market

We touched on your audience and the market in an earlier chapter. Now, we'll dive deep into the potential of the market.

The questions that you might be asked in an application about market potential include:

- Calculate the size of the market you are targeting.
- What percentage of that market do you expect to secure, providing evidence of your calculations?
- What activities have you done to 'test and validate' that your customers want your product?
- How do you plan to scale your business from its current position in the market to where you want to go?

What assessors are looking for

When assessing applications seeking funding to commercialise a new product into a market, assessors want to see that you've spent time preparing future forecasts.

Forecasting and modelling can be daunting even with your business success so far. Because you're making a commitment to deliver, you'll want to be confident that you can rely on the numbers.

Leveraging what we covered in Chapter 13, calculating your market potential requires research and looking for value in the statistics.

Question 2.4: What is the size of the market(s) you are targeting, and what percentage of this market do you hope to secure? Explain how you calculated the percentage of the market you are targeting. Justify your response with quantifiable data.

When preparing your response for **Question 2.4**, here is an approach that might help:

- Understand the industry or industry sector you are operating in;
- Look for reports published by industry associations, government departments, large not-for-profits or large publicly listed companies; and
- Get a sense of the market potential others are quoting in news articles, then break it down into a figure that is viable for your business.

A word of advice: if you are a new business that isn't yet turning a profit and you don't yet have a team, to suggest that you're going to secure 1% of a $4 billion market within the next two years is totally unrealistic.

Instead, look at the market share of your established competitors and then work backwards to calculate what might be possible for you in your current stage of business. Taking a moment to explore a competitor's growth trajectory may also be helpful when creating a growth plan.

Question 2.5: Describe what you have done to test and validate that customers in your target market will pay for your product.

Breaking down the underlying intention of **Question 2.5**, it becomes easier to understand exactly what is required.

Step 1 – Describe what you've done to test your product with your proposed market.

Step 2 – Describe the results of those product tests.

Assessors are looking for evidence of market demand for your product: not just hearsay but quantifiable evidence that an audience is ready and willing to purchase the product.

A helpful hint … See how I used the steps above? I encourage you to consider simplifying your responses by using a format that helps to step out the process you adopted to complete in-market product testing.

Question 2.6: Explain how and why your product is scalable and has potential beyond this initial market.

To answer **Question 2.6** with confidence, I highly recommend that you consider preparing a growth plan. Once you have a plan on a page, no matter how loose it might be, it will help you to clearly articulate the growth targets you're comfortable with.

Some funding applications may even ask you to submit your growth plan as supporting documentation. It will depend on the program team and how much detail they want to provide assessors.

Whether you need to submit a growth plan or not, it is really important to have a plan done. Let's face it … if you are submitting an application to fund your growth, then having a growth plan is 'kinda' mandatory. Otherwise, how else will you know what to include in your project plan?

Advanced Grant Writing Action

Refer to the application template and prepare the remaining responses in the Market Potential section.

As you're working through the questions and preparing your responses, begin the process of checking in with yourself and asking a few clarifying questions. Do you have any unanswered questions floating around in the back of your mind? If yes, write them down to clear space, but also as a reminder to investigate any niggling feelings. You might be surprised by what is uncovered!

Chapter 15
Ready or Not ...

Being market-ready can be subjective if you're not prepared

Technology readiness is a phrase you've possibly encountered in a digital accelerator program or as a tech product founder, but for those who aren't developing tech, let's talk about product readiness in relation to your Product Development Roadmap (PDR).

Product Development Roadmap

Your PDR is the process you're following to develop your product, from ideation to the release of your Minimum Viable Product (MVP), then going beyond the initial release, looking into the future to define a product that stands the test of time. When considering all the phases of your product development, it is important to map them against a timeline. For example, what will your product look like in 6 months', 12 months' or 3 years' time?

PDRs are very, very handy when preparing your funding application because you will inevitably be asked what is different, unique or unusual about your product.

Applications will likely include questions like:

- Provide a brief history of the development of your product;
- Detail the time it has taken to reach this point in the product development journey; and
- What is innovative, unique, and new about your product?

The assumption behind these questions is that you have a detailed knowledge about the landscape of the market including relevant competitive products, but it is also asking you to clearly articulate what is unique about your product when compared to others.

If you've never seen a PDR, take a moment to search online. You'll find quite a range of types and styles of roadmaps available. Some are sophisticated and very detailed. Others are basic. If you're new to the PDR, I encourage you to find a style of map that is easy to understand. To help get you started, I've prepared a downloadable template available as a book-bonus. You can access it via www.funding4growth.io/book-bonuses

Product Readiness Levels

To help explain this concept, please download the Product Readiness guide found via www.funding4growth.io/book-bonuses It highlights the nine stages of readiness within three phases of commercialisation.

Once you've overlayed a timeline to your product development journey, the next step in bringing more clarity to your responses is to refer to the current stage of product readiness captured in your roadmap.

With this level of detail documented, you will easily craft responses with confidence and passion because you are able to draw parallels between the terminology used in program guidelines and what has actually happened in your business.

If you are in a research phase, testing ideas, or developing your proof of concept, and the program guideline states that your product *must be at or beyond MVP,* then you are not yet where you need to be to meet the expectations of the funding program.

Funding programs like BFFI expect the applicant's business is ready to scale, which means the product must already be deployed into a market and often (but not always) in a revenue-generating position.

So, understanding the Product Readiness Levels will significantly help you to:

- Understand the eligibility guidelines; and
- Craft your responses.

What assessors are looking for

Referring back to the application template, look for the section that references Market Readiness, including the following questions:

Question 3.2: Address product development, customer trials and the steps undertaken to reflect customer feedback and prototype status.

Question 3.4: Where do you expect the commercialisation of your product to be at the conclusion of the project (12 months)? Cover market entry, expected customer numbers, projected sales and revenue.

Your response to **Question 3.2** is basically your roadmap overview. You now have the ability to respond to the question using relevant terminology, giving your response the structure it needs against a timeline. This is your opportunity to take the assessor on your product development journey. Be factual. Use real results. Talk to the status of the development, including what is planned next.

Similarly, your response to **Question 3.4** will build on the previous responses by looking further into the future. For example, if your Product Readiness Level is #5 and you've tested market interest by releasing your MVP, and the next level is #6, a pilot project, then your response will need to include projections. Using your baseline numbers, such as the number of beta users you have engaged and their willingness to purchase the product, you then have the ability to extrapolate your numbers to determine how many new customers you are likely to secure and what your future sales revenue will be.

Are you starting to see how each activity builds on the previous?

When you take a step back from the detail and look more holistically at the process, it really is amazing how interlinked everything is. You will also see how application questions are seeking *very specific* responses.

Advanced Grant Writing Action

Refer to the application template and prepare the remaining responses in the Market Readiness section.

Keep in mind that there are elements of similarity in responses. It is important to understand when an overview is requested and when you are asked to dive deep. Do that by leveraging your response to one question as a lead into the next.

As an assessor, I often see applicants simply cut and paste the same responses from one question to another. Please don't do that! As soon as I see an applicant is reusing the same responses, I immediately know they aren't ready for the funding being requested.

Give yourself the best chance of success by putting in the effort to establish your Product Development Roadmap.

Chapter 16
Selling Your Project

Getting the pitch right

If you follow me on the socials or YouTube, you may have heard me talk about the importance of staying away from using technical language or industry jargon when preparing your application responses. But here's the thing ... Sometimes, certain terminology is helpful.

Like in the previous chapter, using the right terminology for the levels of readiness will help you to frame your project-related responses. Especially when presenting your project overview.

Project Overview

The project overview is your elevator pitch for the project, not for your business as a whole. Sure, the spice that is your business should add flavour, but it shouldn't be the spotlight at this time. The project is front and centre.

In preparing a really good project overview, it is important that you build out a full project plan first. Once you've outlined the activities and deliverables for the project against the defined timeline, then you're ready to prepare your overview. It's kind of like preparing an executive summary; these are always written last.

Once you have your project plan prepared, then come back to your project summary and write up your overview. Like your elevator pitch, this overview has to be to-the-point, factual and presented confidently.

Take a look at this example:

ABC Ventures has developed a world-first recycling management system "VeryCoolThingy," consisting of an Internet-of-Things monitoring device, cutting-edge analysis model and an engaging, user-friendly software platform.

It is retrofittable to any recycling operation to generate custom, optimised management instructions that accelerate decomposition speed, minimise pests and eliminate odours during recycling. It also features numerous other engagement and educational functionalities that work together to make recycling accessible to anyone, anywhere.

The funding will enable ABC Ventures to commercialise this innovative technology into the Australian market, provide efficient, affordable waste management to regional areas, create long-term employment both inside and outside the company, and increase waste recycling rates, among numerous other environmental benefits.

At the completion of this project, we will be positioned to commence exporting to international regions, expand into other industry verticals and rapidly scale our HQ and manufacturing capabilities.

Notice how the overview from ABC Ventures summarises the key features of the product first and then explains the potential of what's possible with expansion. After that, it is very specific about how the commercialisation process is expected to benefit the community. In this one response, the foundation is set, and the remainder of the application will build on it by providing more detail.

For the novice applicant, the project overview can trip you up. As an assessor, I've regularly seen a business overview response duplicated for the project overview question. There are similarities between the two, but the project overview focuses 100% on the project you seek to deliver with the funding you're applying for.

Following the project overview is often a question requesting further clarification about what you propose to deliver with the funding, such as *Outline the outcomes you expect to have achieved by project completion*. The detail required for this response will be dependent on the word count, so be sure to keep an eye out for that.

Advanced Grant Writing Action

Before we proceed to the next chapter, think about what your proposed project outcomes might look like, and then be sure they align with the desired program outcomes outlined in the program guidelines.

It is critical that the project you have designed fits perfectly with the funder's goals. A misalignment here will be detrimental to you securing the funding you want. Getting your responses right, however, will set you up for the remainder of the application.

CHAPTER 17
Your Project Viability

What is viability?

In a project sense, when a funding application is asking about your project viability, your responses need to demonstrate how your project is the *level-up* your business needs for long-term, sustainable success.

When outlining your project viability, consider:

- The design of the activities to attract and increase customers;
- Previous attempts to secure external funding; and
- Your pathway to financial sustainability.

Your responses to project viability questions should also leverage any previous successes you've had so that you can demonstrate evidence that points to your ability to deliver what you say you're going to deliver.

One of the easiest ways to demonstrate viability is to have a fully formed project plan at the ready. That way, you can provide summarised information or dive deep into the detail, whatever is required. By including the activities you are planning to complete, proposed outcomes and how they align with the funding budget, you will set your application up for success.

For example:

Activity 1.1 – Commence a promotional campaign in [defined location] to increase take-up of the product.

Activities include digital email campaign, attending [industry-specific] tradeshow, and developing promotional media resources such as flyers, info packs, and tip sheets to secure new customers.

Outcome 1.1 – Product promoted to 33% of all *potential* customers in [defined location] with [xx] new customers secured. Milestone 1.1 – due by July 2023. Budget Allocation – $32,000.

Note: If by spending $32k, you only secure four new, one-off customers for a low-level product, then it is difficult to demonstrate that the project is viable because customer numbers are not sufficient to contribute to the sustainable future of the business.

If by spending $32k, you secure four new five-year contracts for your premium, high-priced product, each contract capturing 400 new customers, then you are demonstrating that the funding investment offered to accelerate further growth taps into a momentum that is already in motion.

Before handing over to you to complete the milestone-related questions in the Project Activities and Proposed Outcomes section of the application, let's take a moment to review the types of activities that may be considered eligible.

Eligible project-related activities

Below is a brief summary of the types of activities that may be appropriate for seeking funding for a project focusing on business growth or commercialisation.

These can include:

- Labour costs for project-related personnel;
- Eligible expenditure for contractors;
- Domestic travel and reasonable accommodation costs;
- Cost of acquiring technology;
- Staff training to build skills directly related to project outcomes; and
- Contingency (usually between 10-20% of total project cost).

Sample ineligible activities include:

- Core day-to-day business expenses (like salaried staff not working on the project);
- Research not directly supporting eligible activities;
- Activities, equipment, and supplies already supported from other funding sources;
- Financing costs, including interest;
- Insurance costs;
- Cost of purchase, development or lease of land or buildings; or
- Cost associated with preparing the grant application.

If in doubt, always reach out to the program team attached to the funding and ask clarifying questions.

Advanced Grant Writing Action

My advice is don't skimp on the detail here. You may be restricted by the word limit in the application, but (as mentioned above) having a fully formed project outline prepared in your draft project plan will help you communicate with ease!

It is 100% easier to reduce the size of your responses because you have too much information than it is to be scrambling to provide enough detail. You don't want assessors with open questions that can't be answered.

Let's not waste time …

Refer to the questions in the application template that specifically ask you to outline your milestones and begin to prepare your methodical, structured responses.

CHAPTER 18
Your Project Outcomes

Set your sights on what you want to achieve

You've prepared your project overview, you understand the importance of demonstrating project viability, and now it's time to delve deep into the proposed outcomes of your project.

In the last chapter on project viability, I laid out an example (Activity 1.1) of how to present project activities, proposed outcomes, milestones and budget allocation. I recommend you consider using this format for all proposed activities and outcomes because using that format will make the transition into the next section of the application template super easy.

Often, the application will ask for a response that is a summarised view of the project outcomes. Too often, I've seen these responses rushed, never quite reaching their full potential.

I've prepared the following examples of rushed versus considered.

Here's a rushed example;

> *First of all, we need to produce our first production model, which will involve employing people in-house to do this. We will need more shed space so will rent the shed next door which recently became available.*

Once we have the production model available, our marketing team will go to work with current interested parties. We have the Port of Hogwarts already mentioning the ability to invest $400,000 into the project along with XYZ Investors to put more devices on the Hermione River.

We will also investigate the current inquiries from Place B, Place C, and Place Q to gain traction. With our prototype having the ability to be moved by road, we may opt to take the prototype to Place R and Place V for trials. However, this type of item is known to go viral and hence I believe we will be inundated with orders and we need to be in a position to take advantage of that quickly.

When you read the sample above, can you clearly see the vision of the project, what it is designed to achieve, and by when?

I couldn't.

For me, this example didn't structure a response using a project management framework. As a result, the project got lost in translation.

In comparison, here's a considered response:

In the six months from July 2021 to December 2021, we will achieve the following key outcomes:

1. By EOM July 21 – Finalise production, including final product design and engineering of two launch products.

2. By EOM August 21 – Finalise a fully tested pricing strategy ready for launch.

3. By EOM August 21 – Finalise packaging design and specifications, with complementary corporate stationery and user instruction manuals for both product versions.

4. By EOM October 21 – Embed a fully tested distribution strategy incorporating both direct and indirect channels to market.

5. By EOM October 21 – Finalise an inventory plan.

6. By EOM October 21 – Launch digital assets, including social media, product videos, press releases and other promotional materials.

7. By EOM November 21 – Product launch into Victoria, New South Wales, Western Australia and South Australia plus early customer trials in New Zealand.

8. By EOM December 21 – Conduct post-launch activities, including post-market research and customer feedback.

See how the second example is easy to follow and very clearly outlines what the proposed outcomes are. The only improvement I would include is actual engagement and sales results. It would also be helpful to include proposed revenue increases.

Leveraging success

I've mentioned this previously, but I'll say it again. Being able to leverage your previous successes is really important because those previous successes become the baseline from which proposed improvements are layered.

When you know the cost to acquire every new customer into your business is $328, as an example, you can begin to forecast growth outcomes that you will likely achieve when injecting additional funding into your business.

For instance, if you've applied for $32,000 in funding to accelerate your growth, then you could easily expect to secure 97 new customers. Assessors want to see that you're also looking for ways to optimise the cost of acquisition. If you can use the $32,000 to onboard 153 new customers, then you've reduced your cost of acquisition down to $209. This is really positive and demonstrates value for money.

For me as an assessor, I love the project outcome responses, because they tell me exactly what the applicant is focused on achieving. I consider these responses to be the backbone of the entire application. If the outcomes are reasonable, well-considered and built on early successes, then I feel more confident in the applicant's ability to deliver.

My advice? Take all the time you need to get these right and be sure to reference all available program resources to confirm your project is aligned with the program goals.

CHAPTER 19
Your Project Budget

Assigning budget to eligible activities

Budgets: you either love them and use them in your everyday life, or you have a tumultuous relationship with them. Some days, they shine their brightest light on your business success, then other days they feel like hovering rain clouds, bleak and grey.

When it comes to the project budget in your funding application, it is important to give it all the love it needs, because it is just as important as the written responses.

Here's why …

The usual scenario is this. It's the last day that applications are accepted. After spending all day (and most of the previous night) devoted to the application, a great deal of time and effort has been spent working on written responses, only to arrive at the budget section of the application with little time left to spare. Applicants often – in their words – *throw a few 'guesstimate' numbers into the table* and quickly hit *submit*, falling to the floor in a puddle of relief that it's all done!

But guess what? Assessors *love* budgets!

If you could see me right now, you would be having a good chuckle. I'm sitting here typing this with the biggest grin on my face because the mere mention of a good budget brings me joy.

You may recall me mentioning this previously. Assessors love to actively support *deserving* businesses with the funding that is available, but because of the high number of applications received, assessors need to be brutal in their assessment and are looking for any potential weaknesses. Unfortunately, the budget is often an area where weaknesses are found.

My advice is to cross-reference your requested funding amount against your project activities and proposed outcomes to make sure they align. Any misalignment here is problematic.

Be sure to take the time to understand how the budget is to be represented. Sometimes, you will be asked to allocate an amount per proposed milestone, similar to the example provided in Chapter 17. Other funding programs will expect summarised line items such as:

- Hire digital marketing specialist – $45,000;
- Digital marketing campaign – $7,500;
- Industry expo/trade show/summit – $4,900;
- Travel and accommodation – $3,290; and

So on …

Most importantly, include only those expense items that are deemed eligible. Allocating budget to non-project-related activities is a sure way to raise assessor concerns. We don't want that!

Be aware of budget caps

Not all programs will impose caps on budget line items, but some programs do. For example, in the BFFI, the maximum salary for an employee, director or shareholder that you can claim through the grant is $175,000 per financial year.

Be sure to double-check program guidelines to confirm if caps apply.

Commitments if successful

Remember, if your application is successful, you may be asked to verify the project budget provided in your application. Evidence such as final invoices for major costs may be requested. If records are not provided when requested, the expense may not qualify as eligible expenditure, which means either a deduction in your funding amount or expectation of a reimbursement back to the funding provider.

The program management team will usually request a final acquittal report. The report template will sometimes be available at the time of application, otherwise, it is provided during the initial onboarding process when signing of the formal funding agreement takes place.

The final report should never include expenditure surprises but instead confirm only eligible expenses completed during the project period.

Advanced Grant Writing Action

One final reminder before you jump across to the application template and begin populating the budget tables provided: follow the three-part checklist on project expenditure.
- Expenditure must be:
- A direct cost of the project;
- Incurred by you for required project audit activities; and
- Incurred between the project start and end date.

If you prefer to work in a spreadsheet rather as opposed to

tables in a written document, simply copy and paste the tables from the template into your preferred tool. Then, once you're done, copy the tables back into the application itself. Whatever works best for you is the right step to take.

Over to you!

CHAPTER 20

Your Organisational Capability

It's not about you; it's about your team

Organisational capability is generally found towards the tail end of the application form. It can also attract a lower assessment weighting by assessors. Even so, it will be taken into consideration during the assessment phase.

When you're a new entrepreneur, it is not unusual to be doing *all the things* yourself. In the early days, there isn't budget available to employ people to come into the business and help. That's okay, and understood.

At this stage of the application, it is important to understand the current phase of your business in terms of Product Readiness Levels. Remember back in Chapter 15 where we covered the phases of business establishment and the different elements within each phase?

If a funding application asks for you to confirm your product is at MVP or beyond, and your application responses suggest that you're ready to begin to scale into domestic (or international) markets, *but* you're still a team of one, assessors will immediately question your organisational capability to deliver the outcomes outlined in your application.

Therefore, if your business is in its very early stage of establishment, then a grant program focused on business growth through scale is not the right fit. You're better to put time into looking for a grant program that is more aligned with your stage of business *and* the capability of your team.

What does organisational capability mean?

Essentially, assessors are looking for confirmation that the *business* has the required skills and expertise to successfully achieve the proposed project outcomes. For example, if one of your project outcomes is to launch into the US market, but you don't have anyone on your team or advisory panel that has successfully done that before, then assessors will notice that gap straight away and note it as a potential risk.

As with other parts of the funding application, organisational capability must cross-reference and be consistent with other elements of your application.

For clarity, refer to the examples shared in Chapter 18. Then it will be easier to align how the team has skills and expertise in the following areas:

- Product design;
- Engineering;
- Packaging;
- Graphic design; and
- Technical documentation and specifications.

Having a fully formed project plan and future vision for your business will help you to respond to the organisational capability questions with confidence.

Building team to grow capability

Some of the best entrepreneurs are great leaders. Great leaders know how to build great teams! Smart businesspeople attract a group of daring doers to help them get it done. Female founders do this so easily and naturally ... because we tend towards collaboration and sharing. We feel strong when we are bringing others on the journey with us.

In my own experience as an entrepreneur, the two biggest challenges when building a team have been having the operational capital and steady cashflow to engage a winning team and choosing teammates wisely.

If your business is on a solid growth trajectory, then assessors want to see that you understand the functions of your business, have realistic growth expectations, plan for sustainable growth, and have embraced your support network.

In case you're wondering, assessors do consider the breakdown of your team whether they are employees, freelancers or contractors. Employees represent more long-term stability in the business. That being said, those assessing your application will also consider the current phase of the business in terms of Product Readiness Levels and therefore look at the following:

- Team competence – the ability to do the work;
- Project commitment – availability to do the work for the defined period of time; and
- Skills connection – ability to leverage the skills of the collective.

As a female founder growing a business, it is important to look beyond those who are your internal, process-orientated, operations-focused team. By inviting others to contribute at a more strategic level, they will help you navigate your way around hidden speed-bumps, which is incredibly important.

When considering the types of strategic roles assessors look for, think:

- Board members;
- Advisory panel;
- Mentors; and
- Coaches.

Your project-related mentors should be successful in the areas of your desired project outcomes. Recruiting those who have walked your path previously is incredibly valuable. Importantly, they know how to look for unexpected problems and have often got a fix ready to go.

A note on advisers

Advisers are different from mentors in that they are contributing very specific knowledge to your business and often fill a position on your formal advisory panel.

Having advisers is especially relevant for entrepreneurs seeking higher levels of grant funding or venture capital. An advisory panel will likely be a pro bono agreement in the beginning, but as your business grows and your cash flow allows for it, paying your advisers (like you would pay for a board) is a realistic expectation.

They are bringing years of experience and expertise to your business. They do that by helping you to implement processes that build efficiencies and increase your impact and profitability. Paying them a stipend will become a no-brainer.

To find the right adviser, you might consider connecting with professional groups like the Advisory Board Centre in Australia. Look for organisations in your country that offer short–course programs for entrepreneurs and professionals who are offering their expertise and experience as advisers.

Take your time. Be diligent when choosing panellists. Alignment is key.

Getting to this stage of the funding application is interesting because crafting responses about team, capability and experience is just another piece in the jigsaw puzzle that further demonstrates how every section and question response is interlinked. The strength of a response deeper in the application will always be impacted by the strength of other, earlier responses.

Being aware of the need to weave the narrative, even in the last questions of an application, is critical. That is why it is important to take a well-planned, structured approach to your responses. Even those small $5,000 grant applications will require confidence that you have a team capable of meeting the essential deliverables.

Your turn …

GETTING STARTED RECAP

Wow ... that was tough, but you made it!

Getting started on your application is intense, so please give yourself permission to take a break at the end of this section and let the knowledge sink in. Rushing into the next section will not deliver the best result.

As I said in the beginning, a grant application worth $100,000 or more might take upwards of 100 hours, so if you're going to do this, it's worth doing well and being confident of success. Practising now also creates a baseline document that you'll be able to use time and again, making it quicker and easier to prepare applications in the future.

Advanced Grant Writing Action
Before progressing to the next section it is really important that you complete your draft application. Without your completed application, the next section, which is stepping you through the process of assessing your draft application, will be redundant.

It's okay that you might not have all the information available to complete your responses (as you would if it was a real application), but imagining it as a real application and giving it your best will definitely help advance your grant writing skills.

A note about the commercial focus of this book

Sure, not every grant program is asking questions that feed into an assessment about your business's commercial strengths and readiness, but an increasing number do – even those funding programs established to support social enterprises and impact businesses. There is a growing global focus on financial sustainability, so knowing key fundamentals like those listed below is critical to your success:

- Your market;
- Product readiness;
- Phase of growth;
- Team capability; and
- Budget impacts.

Your approach versus my approach

Everyone's approach to completing a funding application will likely be different, and that's okay. The most important thing is that you get it done and done to the best of your ability.

My approach to completing applications is to leverage with tools like Trello. I like to break everything down into lists, then cards within lists, so that as I'm capturing some initial thoughts at the same time as breaking down elements of the program and the application. In doing so I note what data or supporting documents I know I have and what gaps I need to fill. This helps me to plan completion of the funding application, just like I would plan to deliver a package of work.

Maybe you're a fan of this approach, or perhaps you're a little more organic. If you prefer to start filling in the application using bullet points as you go, that's also a valid method and is absolutely okay.

I like to group related topics and prepare my responses for all questions in the same category, at the same time. You, on the other hand, might prefer to start with the budget and work your way backwards through the application.

Whatever approach works best for you is the best approach.

An additional word of advice is to incorporate frequent rest periods during the process. Preparing your funding application is an intensive piece of work. It will take large chunks of focused concentration to get it done. Weaving in exercise and rest is just as important as blocking out time in your calendar to work on the application. The kinder you are to yourself during the process of completion, the more enjoyable and satisfying it will be.

What's next?

Well, if I'm honest … this next section is by far my favourite! It is where I lift the veil and share more of my experience as an assessor and the process of how assessors assess.

It is going to *blow your mind*!

See you there.

Step into the Shoes of an Assessor

KEEPING AN OBJECTIVE MIND

The key takeaway from this section is this: funding applications are not a popularity contest. They are not personal. Funding applications are simply a mechanism to capture information that will be used to determine how well your business meets the outlined assessment criteria for funding.

Assessment criteria have been developed to determine if your project activities align with program objectives. It is important to remember that someone, at some time, pitched the program to be funded. When that happened, there were defined outcomes to be achieved. If your application clearly demonstrates how your activities will help the program achieve its goals, then you're starting from a great place. But nothing is guaranteed.

Should you receive a notification saying that your application has been unsuccessful, please remember that it is **the application** being referenced, not you.

Always let the market tell you what they like about your business, product, or service. They are the ones handing over their dollars in fair exchange for what you're offering. Money in the bank from customers will always be a better indicator than any grant application.

Even if your business is growing by healthy margins and you've got new customers coming to you, an application for funding may still be unsuccessful. There are *so many* reasons why. Rather than allow you to think that unsuccessful responses are a direct reflection of you or your business, I'm sharing an overview of assessment to give added perspective.

Secrets to assessment – revealed!

This overview is a mash-up of checklists that I actually use as an assessor for multiple grant and funding programs. Checklists are never shared with applicants. Instead, they are often hidden away (kept secret) by program management teams.

The reason I've put this overview together for you is to encourage an objective mindset. As you move through this next section, it is important that you temporarily disassociate yourself from your business and application **and step into the shoes of an assessor**.

The goal of this section is to step through the assessment process pragmatically and make a final determination on whether your application would rank highly enough on the assessment matrix to receive funding.

Where is your application strong? Where are the weaknesses? Would *you* fund the project you've pitched in the application? Or would you deem it too risky?

Step forward into the next chapters with an open mind and remember to bookmark your overview. Let the fun begin!

CHAPTER 21

Applying an Assessment Score

Simplifying the complex

Allow me to give you some background on my experience as an assessor.

A government agency (I'm not going to share which one) invited me to join one of their assessment panels for a very popular funding program that opens once per year. I am one person on one panel of three to five people, and there may be up to seven other panels. In fact, there could be up to 35 unaffiliated people reviewing applications, completely independently of each other. We don't know who the other assessors are, so there is no chance of collusion.

Assessors are given the exact same assessment criteria and are asked to assess applications against the core objectives of the funding program. Our assessment results are pooled and compared against the other, then majority rules. These practices safeguard against hidden bias, potential conflicts of interest, and unfair practices.

Now that you've got context, let's jump into the nuts and bolts of it.

The Assessment Legend

The table below is an adaptation of a scoring system typically used by assessors.

When stepping into the shoes of an assessor to assess your own draft application, consider each of the assessment criteria holistically, then assign your score from 1 to 5.

1 – Poor	Considered very weak. Does not meet the intent of the program. Insufficient information to inform a considered assessment.
2 – Marginal	Considered weak. The majority of the information provided does not meet the intent of the program. Missing information limiting ability to form a considered assessment.
3 – Satisfactory	Meets some of the program intent but responses are not compelling.
4 – Good	Responses meet program intent. May have potential but responses lack detail/ explanation in some areas.
5 – Exceptional	Meets the intent of the program. Well-presented application with potential strong outcomes.

The Assessment Summary

Once you've *assessed* a section of your draft application, input the score you've assigned in the summary table below.

Assessment Summary						
Assessment Criteria Category						
Include a score between 1 and 5 given for each overarching category.						
	AC #1	AC #2	AC #3	AC #4	AC #5	AC #6	AC #7
1 – Poor							
2 – Marginal							
3 – Satisfactory							
4 – Good							
5 – Exceptional							
	0	0	0	0	0	0	0

Here's a reminder of the overarching assessment criteria presented as key topics.

- AC #1 – Innovation
- AC #2 – Market Potential
- AC #3 – Market Readiness
- AC #4 – Project Viability
- AC #5 – Organisational Capability
- AC #6 – Economic Benefits
- AC #7 – Social Impact

The ultimate goal of this assessment process is to determine whether your application is likely to be funded or not.

After you've assessed each category of the assessment criteria and given each a score, take a moment to consider the overall strength of the application and ask yourself: *Would I give myself the funding requested?*

1 – Overall Poor	Considered very weak. Do not fund.
2 – Overall Marginal	Considered weak. Do not fund.
3 – Overall Satisfactory	Considered average. Invite to apply again in the future.
4 – Overall Good	Considered good. Include in shortlist for further discussion/assessment.
5 – Overall Exceptional	Considered excellent. Definitely fund the application.

As you're working your way through the assessment process, I encourage you make a note of any obvious areas for improvement. This doesn't need to be long-winded, but it will be really helpful to have bullet points to reference a little later as you're rewriting responses.

Advanced Grant Writing Action

As you're preparing to assess your draft application, now is the time to revisit the program guidelines and refresh your memory around why the funding is being offered, including what outcomes the funder wants to achieve.

The assessment process is more than a series of scores you allocate to your application. It is a serious process of determining if the application is strong enough to be funded. The whole point of the activity is to help you draw links between the funder and your business and to assess how well you've positioned your business as a low-risk, high-value funding recipient.

If you're like me and you love a good spreadsheet, I highly recommend preparing your own assessment template to collate your thoughts and ideas on the go!

In the next chapters, we're going to step through each of the assessment criteria in more detail. Ready? Let's go.

CHAPTER 22
Assessment Criteria #1 Innovation

What makes an application innovative?

Innovation has become one of *those* words used regularly to describe a business or a product, but what does it actually mean?

When assessing your draft grant application, innovation describes something unique or new.

New ... as in a new product, service or tool.

Unique ... as in one-of-a-kind, unlike anything else available.

Remember when https://www.vestiairecollective.com/ launched in 2009? At the time, it was considered an innovative service providing the sellers of high-end designer items with an e-commerce marketplace to sell loved pieces with life still in them.

Digital media companies, like Australia's https://www.mamamia.com.au/ are shaking up news and reporting. Subscription boxes like https://www.stitchfix.com/ are changing the way we shop, and https://www.pleasantstate.com/ is changing the way home cleaning products are manufactured.

When assessing your application responses that describe your product, remember that innovative considers newness and uniqueness.

This assessment criteria is focused on the product being commercialised, including how the competitive advantage is protected from duplication in the market. If a funder is going to support your application for funding, they want to be confident that your product has a greater-than-average probability of sustainable financial success.

So, what are we assessing?

In this assessment criteria, we are looking for activities like:

- Processes to validate product within the market;
- Research and development activities completed; and
- Iterations of how the product evolved following market feedback.

Key deliverables might include:

- A competitor analysis;
- User feedback and reviews; and
- Product protection mechanisms (IP, trademarks etc.).

Not every grant program will be assessing innovation. Other programs might simply ask about your product without innovation being specified in the criteria. Even so, you will likely find there is an expectation to explain what is unique about your product, including what sets it apart from others currently in the market.

Advanced Grant Writing Action
For the purposes of this activity, you will have prepared your draft application with innovation in mind. Using the structured scoring process provided, assess how well you

think your responses met the criteria, then allocate a score for that section of the application.

Be sure to capture comments to identify areas that you feel are answered well, also taking time to highlight what could be done to improve.

Remember, this process is all about acquiring a new level of knowledge so that your application responses can evolve from good to great!

Be objective and curious. Adopt a learner's mindset.

CHAPTER 23
Assessment Criteria #2 Market Potential

Let's assess the market and its potential

I really love this assessment criteria, because it is the underlying force of a successful business *and* a successful grant application.

Knowing your market and its potential is fundamental. Getting this criteria right means that you're also getting it right in your business.

Every grant or competition application you complete will expect you to effectively articulate your customer's problem and how your product is solving that problem for them.

All the elements of this assessment criteria are asking you to dive deep to prove how well you know your market and that you have calculated its commercialisation potential for your business.

Here are some of the key underlying themes:

- What is the demand for your product?
- How well does it meet that demand?
- What is the overarching size of the market?
- What is the possible reach into that market with the

business model you've chosen?

- How well have you calculated your projected market share?

Supplementary items such as letters of support are important, as they introduce external validation of what you've already stated in your responses. Please know that assessors do read the supporting documentation.

In this criteria, assessors are also look for evidence of customer trials and market engagement. We're looking for activities that suggest you've gone to the market, asked them to test what you're offering, and they've provided feedback to help evolve or improve your product.

We're looking for:

- Pricing models that have been tested;
- Distribution channels assessed; and
- Customers starting to purchase.

Advanced Grant Writing Action

As with the previous criteria, work your way through the market potential questions in assessing your draft application, and give your responses an overall score using the tables provided.

Remember to also capture comments on what was strong and what needs more work. More on this in the next section where we'll look at the comments you've collated and how they feed into a reworked application.

CHAPTER 24

Assessment Criteria #3 Market Readiness

This one is a little tricky

Market readiness is often portrayed subjectively. That is because entrepreneurs will assess *their* readiness to sell rather than looking at the opportunity from the perspective of the market.

Assessors are looking for indicators that the market is signalling to you, the business, that *people* are ready to buy what you're offering. For example, one of the questions assessors ask is: *Are the testing and trials of the product appropriate?* This question often has founders asking: *What is 'appropriate' and what does that mean for my product?*

In response to that query, it depends on the product and the market. If your product is an ingestible food, vitamin or medicine, then there is an expectation that significant testing and trials have been completed in alignment with appropriate safety standards and compliance regulations. If your product is a technology tool, then there is an expectation that a solid amount of time has been spent engaging with users and having them test the product, inviting them to come back to you with feedback, which is used to iterate the product development.

Other questions to ask yourself as you're assessing include:

- Would additional testing or product trials strengthen application responses?
- Do the outcomes of product testing strengthen the application, or do they weaken it?
- If the product is defined as being at MVP stage, has that been clearly articulated?
- Do application responses demonstrate that the product has progressively improved?
- What else could be provided in responses to remove ambiguity or confusion?

Advanced Grant Writing Action

To accurately assess this response against the criteria, I encourage you to search a similar successful product in the market and get a sense of what their process was for testing market readiness. Then, gently compare your results against theirs.

Give your responses a score, and write out your comments. Then, move on to the next assessment criteria.

CHAPTER 25

Assessment Criteria #4 Project Viability

Viable by whose measure?

In this chapter, we'll take an objective look at the project outlined in your draft application for funding, then assess … is it viable?

When assessing viability, one of the key underlying principles relates to its level of commercialisation. You might remember in Chapter 17 I highlighted that even if your business is a social enterprise or a not-for-profit, in the world of funding there is a requirement to demonstrate financial sustainability.

Stepping into your assessor persona, two key questions to ask yourself as you're reviewing the project viability section of the application are:

- Does the project align with commercialisation objectives and milestones?
- Will the product be commercially available in the market by the end of the project?

If your project term is 12 months, another key question to consider is:

- Will the project activities outlined during that 12-month

period result in the product being comfortably *in market* and generating promising sales numbers?

In the end, viability is self-sufficiency and growth:

- How do the actions proposed in the project outline translate into measurable results?
- Are sales forecasts robust? Is the pricing model solid? Are margins believable?

The viability of the project outlined in your application is determined by looking at the planned actions against projected outcomes. Are they achievable? Will they help your business become stronger and more able to grow?

Let's talk about scale

One of the key objectives of the sample funding program we've reviewed is scale. You might find it surprising to know just how many grant programs are looking for scale from their applicants.

So, what is scale? Like a musical scale scaling your business in an ordered ascension of increasing pitch (*sales*). Keywords here are ordered and increasing.

As an assessor, I'm looking for a methodical process of increasing results.

In startup land, scale is often thought of as the ability to achieve those increasing results against a decreasing cost of operation. That is, selling more without increasing the cost to sell.

That is why digital technologies have become so popular; once the tech product is developed, the cost to maintain it remains pretty much the same, no matter how many customers are using the tool.

Back to your assessment process.

Advanced Grant Writing Action

Remember to be objective.

Give yourself permission to pull apart your application responses and consider how risk-free your project is.

Record your score for this section, then move on to the next criteria.

CHAPTER 26
Assessment Criteria #5 Organisational Capability

Looking beyond you as a founder

This assessment criteria encourages the assessor to look beyond the founder and their individual capacity to be a successful entrepreneur and to consider the team and its ability to deliver results.

Something that will always differentiate an excellent application from a good one is the way in which founders leverage the holistic capability of the organisation. This is all about the team supporting the founder, helping to achieve sustainable success.

When reviewing your application responses for this section, consider the following:

- Do you have an external panel of advisers?
- What experience do your advisers have that clearly demonstrates their ability to grow successfully funded businesses?
- Does your team have the skills and experience needed to deliver the planned and funded project?
- Is your internal team strong with deep with experience in the field or market you are commercialising into?

- Have you clearly articulated previous achievements of the team as they align to the documented project outcomes?

When considering your responses, take a moment to think about how they could be strengthened:

- Have you included enough information to build confidence?
- Are you using terminology that is easily understood?
- As you're building your team, are you thinking far enough in advance for the skills needed as your business grows, say, in 12 or 24 months' time?

There is no right or wrong way to build strong capability within a team, but if this assessment process has brought a question or two to the surface, then that's a good thing.

Entrepreneurs with high-growth businesses are often caught up in the day-to-day operational details, and it can be difficult to carve out time to *stop and reflect*.

Advanced Grant Writing Action
After assessing the organisational capability in your draft application, I invite you to ponder these questions: What does your dream team look like? Who do you want on the team and why?

Write down whatever inspiration bubbles up! It might just be the beginning of your next recruitment plan.

CHAPTER 27

Assessment Criteria #6 Economic Benefit

Oh ... the good ol' economic benefit question

Assessing this question is soooo subjective because – let's face it – how many founders have had the time or money to complete their own research and evolve that data into economic benefits modelling?

I can tell you. Very, very few.

For one of my businesses, I thought I'd kick off a research project to validate some of my assumptions and confirm what I believed to be true in my market. But ... WOW! Accessing a range of datasets was going to cost anywhere from $35,000 to $150,000, and that didn't include the cost of the research team. Adding the cost of data scientists it was going to be a $300,000 project. Honestly, with $300,000, I could take the business global and not worry about applying for the $100,000 grant I was investigating.

When assessing this criteria, assessors are looking for indications that your business could become a powerhouse employer of people. As I assess applications, I look for the ripple effect. I'm looking for businesses that – by solving a problem –directly *and* indirectly empower others to find employment or businesses that streamline their operations to reduce costs and employ more people.

It's never just about your business. It's about the impact you're having on others in your ecosystem. That's what I love about this criteria. It's an opportunity to think big and look beyond your operational footprint.

As you're reviewing your responses, consider the following:

- Have you clearly demonstrated that by commercialising your product, you are tapping into unrealised opportunities in others, helping them become stronger contributors to economic sustainability and financial success?
- What evidence, data or reports have you referenced to reinforce your calculations and predictions?

Advanced Grant Writing Action

As you review your responses for this criteria, be sure to take a moment and consider the ripple effects of your commercial activities. Start a list of regular beneficiaries of your business and assign an approximate commercial value against them. Then consider the next level down. For example:

- A bookkeeper earns approximately $6,000 from your business engagement
  - As a result, the bookkeeper is able to expand their team by two personnel because of systems they've implemented through having your business as a client

This is a very loose example and it may not be relevant to your funding application, but it serves to explain the ripple effect. The underlying point here is to think about how your funded project will trigger further impact on the economy.

CHAPTER 28
Assessment Criteria #7 Assessing Impact

Looking beyond profit

If you have founded a purpose-driven business, having an impact will be top of mind for you as it is likely woven into the fabric of why your business exists.

However, if your business is considered more 'traditional' in the way it operates, with the primary focus being commercial profitability, that's okay, and there's no judgement from me. In fact, I'd like to see more women entrepreneurs elevate the need to generate a profit. Because without a profit, your business will cease to be viable.

This section is focused on assessing impact and assess impact we shall!

For the purposes of this activity, let's narrow the focus to social impact. To assess all impact would require a whole book. Maybe that's what I'll write about next!

When considering how your project, and by default your business, is impacting others in society, review your application responses from the following perspective:

- Will the project deliver meaningful results to society (outside of the benefit to the applicant organisation)?
- If yes, how so? What evidence has been provided to support claims?
- Does the project have the potential to positively contribute to achieving the United Nations Sustainable Development Goals, or similar?

An acknowledgment of your impact

While not every business is considered to be an impact business, we are an evolving society, which means our businesses will consistently evolve as well. With this evolution comes a requirement to be more aware. Entrepreneurs are being called upon to consider how every element of their business is represented in society. Whether it be the people you employ, the customers you serve, or the suppliers of your products, each level in your product value chain will touch people.

Let's take this book as an example. My hope is that it will trigger a ripple of more female founders applying for and successfully securing $100,000 or more in funding. The more female business owners understanding how grant funding is awarded, the more women will feel empowered to apply; the more funding requested by female business owners, the more successful they will be in securing funds, and in turn, the more women with strong, growing businesses, the more people they will employ.

This book will help increase the flow of money to entrepreneurs who are worthy, with meaningful businesses, that positively impact the world we live in.

Advanced Grant Writing Action

Using the ripple effect concept covered in the previous chapter, consider your application responses and identify ways in which your business is the catalyst of a ripple.

Do you currently measure your impact? If not, what type of measurement framework would be most appropriate for your type of business and the customers you serve? What actions could you take to improve your impact and the way you measure it?

You may not have the answers to these questions now, but maybe in the future, you will

CHAPTER 29
Mapping Weaknesses to Strengths

Weaknesses don't need to remain weak

One of the real benefits of stepping into the shoes of an assessor is taking an objective view of the areas of your application need strengthening.

It also gives you the permission to take a step back and ask yourself a few key questions:

Is it the application that needs tweaking or elements of your business?

Do you need to consider aspects of the business that may have been overlooked?

Is the grant program the 'right' fit for your business and its goals?

Tweak away!

If it is the application that needs tweaking, then take a moment to sit with the weaknesses identified and commit to identifying ways to strengthen the application.

- What data could add value? Where can you source it?
- Could you present the information differently?
- Do you need to collect evidence to support your claims? Where and how?

Whatever it is, once you know what you need, it's incumbent on you to take the next steps to initiate, iterate and improve.

Business review

If you've identified weak areas in your business itself, that can be disappointing and maybe even confronting, but – wow! – isn't that also a wonderful outcome of this process? Rather than continue on the same path, doing the same thing, you've identified an opportunity to reset.

Every business, no matter how big or well-established, has opportunities to improve. Your business is no different.

Growing any business is nothing more than a series of iterations or evolutions. The positive takeaway uncovered by this assessment process is that you've got a clearer understanding of what the next evolution could, or should, be, and now you can plan for it.

Funding pivot

If by the end of this assessment process, you're convinced that this type of grant opportunity is not a good fit for your business, then you have the following options available:

1. Look for a different type of funding program – one that isn't so focused on commercial growth but instead is more community-orientated or impact-led.

2. Consider a different type of funding product. Maybe grants aren't the right choice for your business, so look for equity funding, revenue-based financing, business loans or corporate competitions.

My hope is this …

When an assessor identifies what is perceived to be a weakness in your application or business, you now know *at your very core* that it is a strength waiting to be uncovered and nurtured. Isn't it wonderful to have clarity about where to direct your attention?!

Advanced Grant Writing Action
What will you do differently next time?

Take a moment to reflect on your draft application and consider the suggestions included in this chapter. Will you:
- Tweak your application?
- Look for a different grant program?
- Look for a different type of funding product?
Maybe you'll consider all three, and that's okay too!

Revamping 4 Success

AVOIDING COMMON PITFALLS

As an assessor, I can tell you this ...

I want as many women entrepreneurs as possible to apply for the money they need, and to receive that money. I am actively cheering for you as I'm assessing. I want you to be successful.

Through the process of stepping into the shoes of an assessor, you now understand that assessors need to be impartial with their assessment. Every decision we make to record a strength or weakness must be justified with detailed comments.

For example, if I am assessing applications for a commercialisation or business innovation grant, then fundamental to the whole assessment process is this question:

> **If this applicant receives the money they are requesting to commercialise their product, will receiving the money achieve that goal?**

Your objective as an applicant is to *clearly demonstrate* to assessors that your product is ready and the funding being requested will deliver the outcomes outlined in the application and project plan.

Here's the thing ... Demonstrating that your business is a worthy recipient of the funding can take on more subliminal characteristics as well, and that's the focus of this next section.

We've done the hard yards in the previous sections by focusing on the data, success measures, project planning and all the heavy stuff. Now we get to have some fun!

Continue onto the next chapter for my helpful hints in taking your grant application beyond good ... to *exceptional*!

CHAPTER 30
The Power Shot

The secret to leading strong

Have you ever tried a pure shot of ginger? Wow ... it is strong ... it wakes you up ... and it burns!! But after throwing it back, you are 100% energised, alert and ready for whatever comes next.

Wanna know a secret?

I equate the first long-form question response in grant applications as a ginger shot that you deliver, and the Assessor gets to consume. Generally, that first long-form question is some form of 'tell us about your business.' That question is often supported with helpful suggestions like provide details about:

- Your product;
- Your primary target audience; and
- The size of your market.

These pointers are good, but they don't convey how important this first response is.

It is your power shot.

Your first long-form response is your opportunity to lead strong.

To set the theme for the remainder of the application. To prove that you're here and you're a contender.

Here are a few examples of first responses, given a 50-word response limit:

> _Purely Polished_ is a marketplace to book on-demand manicures and pedicures, to your door, anytime, anywhere.

> _Littlescribe_ is an education platform solving the world's literacy challenges. Children are empowered to create and publish their own books. It is a platform where children's writing is used as a teaching tool that connects cultures and communities.

Here's a slightly longer response with a 100-word limit:

> _Crockd_ is commercialising the concept of 'Creative Mindfulness' for distributed global teams. Crockd is a creative mindfulness platform designed to connect remote employees by enabling them to get 'out of their heads and into their hands.'

> We do this through a specifically designed curriculum of creative experiences for diverse workforces. The experiences themselves are supported with Crockd's own branded, and self-manufactured supplies, bringing a virtual experience into the physical realm.

> We've tested this MVP over the last 12 months with our partners at Google, Shopify, Meta, The New York Times, Canva, Atlassian and others.

Let me be clear. All of these responses are good. They all articulate what the product is and who the market is, but ...

- Which one of the three above inspires you to read further?
- Which has you feeling excited about what the rest of the application has in store?

That is what your power shot does. It has the reader thinking to themselves, _Ooh, tell me more._ This immediately puts the assessor into *the flow* of your application. They are *in sync* with you and the narrative you are creating for them. They are being led to the destination of your choice.

It is important to remember the power you have in your hands, through your words. Own it.

CHAPTER 31
Reading Speed

Reading for inspiration

Did you know ...?

A normal reading rate for learning is 100-200 words per minute. For comprehension, it is **200-400 wpm**. Speed reading is normally done at a rate of around 400-700 wpm. Anything above 500-600 wpm means sacrificing comprehension, although this varies from person to person.

Adults typically read at about 300 wpm when reading fiction for enjoyment, but reading speed will also depend on the type of book or material. For example, technical material such as operating manuals, manual repair guides, or complicated scientific research typically requires more focus and attention to detail, which can slow reading speeds down to 125 wpm.

You may not have ever considered this, but assessors want to feel joy when they are reviewing funding applications. They want to feel the energy of your business. To be inspired by what you're delivering. They want to become your advocate.

The reading speed of your responses is important.

Take a moment to think back to the last book that you read – before this one!

- Was it good? If it was good, what did you like about it? If it wasn't, why did you keep reading? Or did you give up and put it back on the shelf?
- How quickly did you finish it? Did time fly, or did it drag on?
- Was it one of those books that you just couldn't put down and *needed* to find out what happened? Was it something you only read because you wanted the information? Was it hard to get through? Did it entice you from the first page?

When assessors are randomly allocated a great application to review, the experience is just like a good book. You can't wait to read the next response!

One of my favourite tools

Because I'm a techno-geek, I love using digital tools to assist me with improving my work, so I'm going to share one of my favourites!

Allow me to introduce … https://hemingwayapp.com/

The Hemingway Editor will assess your written work by grading it as easy or difficult to read. It will also highlight areas for improvement. It looks at your sentence structure, makes grammar suggestions, helps you avoid the passive voice, mitigates too many adverbs, improves the fluency of your writing and enhances basic sentence structure. The use of passive voice, too many or weak adverbs and low-modality language is common – way too common! – in applications prepared by women. Application responses seem apologetic rather than confident and assured.

What do I mean by this terminology?

Passive voice - to be clear, voice in this instance is referring to the grammatical quality of the verb – not the voice or personality you are using as the writer.

You know you are using passive voice when the tone in your response is sublter, wordier, lacks clarity and feels detached. As an Assessor reading passive responses, I can feel how the applicant has stepped away from the question and is trying to hide behind filler words or simply lacks confidence..

This is not how you want assessors to feel about your application, so here are a few signposts of passive voice to look for and consider rewording to active voice:

- phrases that contain a "to be" verb such as was, were, has been, will be;
- these are often followed by a "-en" or "-ed" form of verb e.g. "was completed", "has been achieved", "will be built" or "is being tested";
- sentences starting with "it is" or "it was"; and
- "by the" phrases.

Here is an example[11] to clarify:

Passive voice: Gender and annual income were cited by the research as the major drivers of purchase decisions.

Active voice: The research cited gender and annual income as the major drivers of purchase decisions.

Becoming more aware and deliberate about which voice you use will impact the style and tone, as well as clarity of your application and ensure your writing sounds compelling, concise and direct.

---

11 reference: https://www.forbes.com/sites/laurambrown/2019/05/10/whats-the-big-deal-about-the-passive-voice/?sh=6390c96f48e7

Adverbs are words that describe or qualify verbs and tell you how, where, when, why an action is carried out. In application responses they appear as words like – slowly, frequently, partially, probably, certainly, obviously, surely, only, generally, mainly, largely, often, sometimes, usually, really and just.

Don't overuse adverbs as you risk boring your reader; instead, consider substituting with a strong adverb. Using strong adverbs in your application writing makes it more precise, punchy and powerful.

Modality[12] is a linguistic term that describes words or phrases that convey the level of certainty or degree of obligation around an action.

Low modality language, as the name implies, carries uncertainty and doubt and is inherent in words like *maybe, perhaps, try, could, should, might, possibly, somewhat, hope, potentially* and *generally*. High modality language, on the other hand, instills confidence, certainty and intensity. By incorporating high-modality words such as *integral, important, evident, definite, clear, vital* and *necessary* in your application writing, you will more likely be perceived as strong, confident and assured.

If you want to see what a powerful effect it has, compare these two paragraphs:

> *Collaborations with remarkable brands such as Canva, Atlassian, Salesforce, Tiffany & Co. have been engaged in by us. Our work, it is worth noting, has occasionally found itself being featured in publications like The Sydney Morning Herald, The Daily Mail, and Channel 7's Sunrise.*

Instead, consider…

> *We've collaborated with incredible brands like Canva, Atlassian, Salesforce, Tiffany & Co. The Sydney Morning Herald, The Daily*

---

12 reference: https://artofsmart.com.au/english/high-modality-words/

Mail, and Channel 7's Sunrise have featured our work.

The difference between the two sentences isn't overtly obvious, but when reading them aloud, you can feel how the second is punchier and more direct. I'd love to see more applications from female founders where responses are unapologetic in their confidence.

That is why I'm suggesting Hemingway Editor. When you see a passage of text and it is as colourful as the rainbow, you will immediately know there are improvements to be made. My rule of thumb is to have paragraphs without colour and to have zero sentences that are hard to read.

When it comes to preparing grant application responses, this app changed my life. I promise it will change yours too!

Try it. You'll see. You're very welcome!

Advanced Grant Writing Action
Choose one of the smaller word limit responses from your draft application and drop it into the app.

I wish I could see your face right now! I'm confident you're frowning as much as I did when I first used the tool. Once you get over the initial shock of all the red, yellow, purple, blue and green highlights, it's amazing how quickly you adapt because nothing beats seeing a reading level of Year 9 or below!

Ready for more? Let's talk jargon!

CHAPTER 32
Sophisticated Simplicity

Avoid buzzwords at all cost!

I cannot tell you how many applications I've reviewed that try to dazzle me with their technical prowess. In the end, those applications annoy me because the language is impenetrable and they take ages to read and wrap my head around. As a result, I inevitably assess responses as weak, often because I'm so aggravated.

I do not want to read a technical manual or your research paper. I want a concise and succinct application for funding.

Here's a typical annoying example:

> Our 'special sauce' is that we combine data from very different domains (code, cloud, assets) and bring that data together into our own proprietary logic engine. There are other tools out there that do these different things individually, but there is no other product combining all three types of data to make insights. Moreover, we use that unique insight to give the customer-specific recipes or discreet automation to fix the problem we helped them find. Those suggestions are typically very targeted, as Product B understands the customer's application in a way that no other tool does, because it *does* use the different types of data to come to its conclusions. For example, because we understand

that an application is running on a Linux server in AWS and that it has a security flaw, we can help the customer understand how to implement a fix in AWS that will mitigate the security flaw.

When I read an application response, I want to know what is innovative about this product and why the market wants it. Therefore, they could have said...

We capture data generated from your codebase, your cloud hosting platform, and your live software application and assess it for cyber security risks. Once a risk is identified, our tool will not only notify you of the potential problem but also offer suggested mitigations or controls to reduce the likelihood of it becoming a real security issue. Other products in the market will look for security risks, one asset at a time, but without a holistic view of the full end-to-end process, including how each asset intersects with the other, potential security issues are missed. These missed risks cost technology-dependent businesses $xxx,xxx in lost uptime and upwards of $xxx,xxx if a data breach was to happen.

See the difference?

I'm not using jargon. I removed the techie speak. What I communicated was clear, to-the-point, and embraced my approach of using **sophisticated simplicity**.

Structure your responses using language that demonstrates you know what you're doing, that you're an expert in your field, and that you know what makes your business stand out. When you are articulate in your approach, there is power in your confidence.

Use understated bling!

"Before you leave the house, look in the mirror and take one thing off. It is always better to be underdressed." – Coco Chanel

Like all assessors, I want to be inspired by how you are delivering a solution to a market that is looking for what you're offering. I want to be confident that you can deliver what you say you're going to deliver, within the timeframe allocated and for the budget requested.

If you're building a technology tool that uses machine learning, that's fine. Tell me once and don't tell me again!

It is important not to confuse the underlying meaning of the word *innovation* when used in assessment criteria. Innovation, in the world of grants and funding, will often mean novel, new to market, not being done elsewhere. It means, for example, that AI or machine learning is not necessarily considered innovative, especially if 15 other applicants are building similar technology tools all using the same pre-trained learning models.

Demonstrating that you know what your market wants, and you're supplying it to them in the way they want to consume it, is by far the most important thing.

Advanced Grant Writing Action
Refer back to your draft application and look for a wordy response that you identified as one with development potential, then pull it apart by identifying all the jargon or buzzwords.

How can you replace those surplus words with a more succinct phrase that communicates clearly without the reader needing a PhD in your industry?

The Hemingway Editor will kickstart this process, but it will be up to you to drill down further and remove anything that is white noise.

Once you've done that with one of your responses, consider how you can use this approach with your website copy or your marketing messaging.

Powerful, isn't it?

CHAPTER 33
Narrate the Journey

It's more than telling a story

If you've been exploring grants for some time, I'm confident you will have seen advice that talks about *telling the story* of your business. It's good advice. But I want you to up the ante.

I want you to think of yourself as the narrator of the journey. That is, the journey of your business from startup through each development phase into becoming a fully functional commercial enterprise focused on making a sustainable profit in years to come.

Remember in Chapter 15 when we explored the Product Development Roadmap? Now is a suitable time for a refresher on that phased process.

When taking your idea to market and building a business, the process of bringing new products to market is the process of commercialisation. It includes production, distribution, marketing, sales, customer support and all the other key functions required to achieve commercially sustainable success.

In startup land, the commercialisation pathway is incredibly important.

- How was the idea birthed?
- Who has tested it?
- Have you achieved market validation?
- What has been the process of evolution, getting from idea to MVP?
- How much is the market willing to pay?

To answer any (and all) of these questions you need to engage with your market. Allow them to guide you in what they want and why they want it.

Then let that *process of engagement* be the story you narrate.

The narration is less about you, or what motivates you, and instead shines the spotlight on your audience and how they benefit from your product.

Starting at the beginning of your application, your first response will set the theme for the remainder of the submission, with the story arc building to the proposed project deliverables and aligned budget. If the funding program you're applying to also asks for economic or social benefit outcomes, then these become the epilogue to the story – future-casting what is possible, using solid data-driven evidence.

Here's one example of how to set the theme:

> *We have developed a product that has been tested and validated close to expected performance, but it is not substantially in market and needs further development. Multiple stages of product development have been completed, including extensive research, in-school trials, and customer testing.*
>
> *During the development process, we gathered feedback from both teachers and students to ensure that the system meets their needs and is user-friendly.*
>
> *Pilot tests were conducted on 40 students in [this awesome school] experiencing varying levels of dyslexia, to assess the effectiveness of our*

program. Based on customer feedback and test results, improvements were made along with adjustments to the system, to ensure that it met the needs of our target audience.

This iterative process allowed us to create a product that is effective, user-friendly and tailored to the needs of children with dyslexia.

Here's an equally good response, presented differently.

Platform A is the premier platform for job seekers. Put simply, our technology exists to turn job seekers into job-getters.

Using machine learning and AI we not only match people to the jobs they want, but Platform A also provides feedback on every single job application giving job seekers a chance to understand what they can do to improve their chances.

We partner with job seeker advocates and employers, the broader job market, as well as educators and industry to help communities anticipate labour demand, lift employment rates and solve skills gap.

We believe that everyone, regardless of gender, race, ability or age has the right to a job – and not just any job, but a job they love. Supported by the Department of Jobs Growth, we have recently adapted our platform to address the unique needs of disengaged young people as well as those with a disability.

Advanced Grant Writing Action
Refer to the draft application, specifically (3.2) Address product development, customer trials and the steps undertaken to reflect customer feedback and prototype status.

This is your opportunity to review the response you originally provided and now reflect on how well it narrates the journey from idea to current state.

- How could you describe the development process better?
- Does the narration incorporate enough input from your customers, in the form of tester feedback?
- As the product has iterated and evolved, what have been the key significant learnings that inspired changes or pivots that have brought you to this point?

Even though I'm asking you to consider how you've narrated the product development journey, in reality, if you were to step back from each individual question and its associated response, and take a more holistic view, the whole application *should* give the assessor a complete experience. Starting with what the product is, who wants it and why, leading all the way through the ups, *and the downs* and the pivots to land where you have in communicating your growth plan – the steps you're taking to build momentum and long-term sustainability.

A final word on story

Don't be afraid to narrate your business's journey to success. In fact, I encourage you to embrace this opportunity to future-cast, to visualise the future of your business and envision its success, including the steps you took to get there.

That's the story assessors want to read.

CHAPTER 34
Data, Insights and Research

Showcasing with facts and numbers

You may have already arrived at this conclusion, but in case you haven't … including data and analytical insights in your application responses is incredibly powerful.

Assessors are looking for confirmation that you've completed an appropriate amount of research. And I'm not talking about desktop research. I'm referring to 'getting out into the wild' type of research.

Sure, allocating time to research is a commitment and is quite an effort, but I can guarantee that applications with data and insights derived from research activities stand out from those applications submitted by people who have not given attention to this aspect of their business and product development.

Types of data

The types of data you might consider collecting and keeping track of, include:

- How much it costs to acquire a customer;
- What your financial return is for every customer acquired;

- Product user feedback, what they liked, didn't like, and want more of;
- Trials or activities that demonstrate how you tested your pricing model;
- Ways you've tested delivering your product/service to your market;
- Profit margins (always handy to know, but not always needed in applications); and
- Size of the addressable market, against the size of the attainable market.

Using the 'best guess' approach will damage your chances of funding success because guesses are often accompanied by vague language.

> For example, ***a large percentage*** *of the market wants a subscription pricing model providing* ***a significant profit*** *back to the business.*

These words tell me the applicant is clueless: *a large percentage, a significant profit*. As an assessor, I want you to tell me how large that percentage is in actual figures, and the same for the rate of profit.

If you can, provide demonstratable insights such as:

> Of the 76 users surveyed, 83% said they wanted to 'immediately' sign-up for our $33/month subscription and the remaining 17% was a mix of 'not interested' and 'want more information'. Achieving a benchmark of 36 new users every month on the base subscription will achieve financial break-even.

Do you see the difference? Can you feel the power in the second response using real figures? I can assure you that assessors feel it too.

Is there such a thing as too much data?

Some would say yes, but I'm of the opinion that while all data is helpful, its usefulness depends on the question asked.

If you are new to collecting data and looking for analytical insights, I encourage you to start by asking your customers for regular documented feedback. Surveys are great but so are polls. Whatever feedback makes sense for your business is worth seeking out, as long as you keep track of the numbers.

Regularly look at your results and get a sense of the story the market is telling you. I am always looking for *signals* in my data. What is working, what is not, what needs modifying, and what is ready for expansion?

When you stop to look, I hope you're pleasantly surprised by what you see. If not, that's okay too. There's always time to implement a new process that adds ongoing, long-term value to your business.

Advanced Grant Writing Action
Take a step back from individual responses in your draft application and make your way back to the beginning.

Read each question again. As you do, identify the questions that are obviously asking for data. Take a moment to look for the questions with the following words or phrases:
- Outline the outcomes;
- Outline the key findings of your research;
- Outline the research and analysis to identify your target audience;
- Outline the key findings and market statistics;
- Justify the share of the market being targeted;
- Outline testing and findings; or
- Outline expected customer numbers and projected sales in 12 months.

Even the section highlighting the project plan and associated budget is stronger when data is woven throughout because it will highlight the baseline from which you're starting. That way, when you're communicating *growth figures*, they are meaningful when compared to known data.

One of the hardest parts of analysing data and insights is starting the process. If this is new to you, I recommend beginning with one element of your business and recording your findings in a spreadsheet. Using worksheets for data makes it so much easier to apply formulas for calculations and projections.

There's no need to overwhelm yourself with this. One small step, regularly is an excellent approach.

CHAPTER 35
Respecting Timelines and Due Dates

Reverse-engineering is your new best friend

If you've applied to a grant program before, you'll know that most programs will be offered in *rounds*, which means there will be an opening and closing date for accepting applications.

Typically, you might find that rounds open for anywhere between three weeks and three months. Other programs – and one in particular that I'm aware of – is open for as long as it takes to exhaust the funding available, on a first-come first-served basis. In 2022, it was open for only 90 minutes before it closed. Others are open for years before closing.

What am I saying here?

Be sure to investigate the program so you know exactly when it opens and when it will close. If you're not organised enough to know these key dates and times, then you're significantly reducing your likelihood of funding success. That's a big statement, I know.

That is why I love reverse-engineering!

Start from the end date, and then work your way backwards to give yourself every opportunity for success. I love using workflow management tools like Trello for this exact reason. By breaking down all the tasks required to build your application, you can set deliverable dates for each element required.

This process also guards against the habit that so many people fall into, which is leaving the preparation of their applications to the last minute. This strategy *never* goes well and is often the critical point of failure for submissions that would otherwise be exceptional.

When rushing to get an application submitted, key pieces of information will be omitted, supporting documents remain unfinished (if they were ever started), and responses thrown together without thought or strategic intention.

As an assessor, I can tell within the first few responses if someone has left their application to the last minute. Responses are grammatically poor, often with typos everywhere, and sentence structure is so bad it can take me three or four read-throughs to really understand what the applicant is trying to say. If I'm having to decipher your first responses, then I can reasonably assume the whole application will lack structure, use poor formatting, and have responses that miss the point.

Now that you've been through the assessment process yourself, you can see that applications considered *good* may still miss out on funding, especially when there are considerable *exceptional* applicants.

I am not kidding. That is how competitive these grant programs are. One poorly worded response is enough to drop you down in the ranking and significantly impact your chance of success.

> **Advanced Grant Writing Action**
> To set yourself up for success, be sure to give yourself time to plan, do and review.
> 1. Plan what is needed and by when;
> 2. Take action with the intention to deliver on time; and
> 3. Give yourself the space to review your work, because I guarantee you'll want to tweak it for improvement.
>
> Oh, and one last bit of wisdom ... set yourself the goal to have your application submitted at least 24 hours before the closing day and time.

Here's why...

As the majority of applications are online, you will need to upload your responses and submit the final application using an online portal. When most applicants are rushing to submit their applications in the final 24 hours, without fail, the portal will crash. If it doesn't crash, it will certainly be running slowly. There is a risk of your application taking too long to load. Even if an application is partially uploaded, the portal will automatically close at due time. You'll be shut out of contention.

Please don't do that to yourself.

The stress and pressure you're subjecting upon yourself is unnecessary.

Give yourself permission to prioritise the preparation of a winning application, by allocating an appropriate amount of time to the task at hand.

I promise it will be worth the effort.

CHAPTER 36
My Biggest Secret

It's so easy, but it will take courage ...

My biggest secret when preparing a grant application for submission is this: **peer review**.

Sounds easy enough, but surprisingly, few people seek input from someone in their circle of trust. On the flip side, sometimes those who are asked to perform the review feel bad offering up feedback that could be considered a criticism or negative in nature, so they soften their feedback so much that it becomes useless.

Now that you've tasted what it's like for an assessor look for a trusted accountability partner to perform the review using the assessment structure (or some form of it).

If you don't want that level of review, a simpler process is to share a draft copy of your application in a Google Doc and ask a reviewer to add comments directly into the document. Ask them to review based on simple logic:

- What is confusing or doesn't make sense?
- Can they call out the use of buzzwords that lack meaning?
- Can they clearly see how your application meets program objectives?

Even if the review stays at a high level, just having someone proofread your application will always pick up spelling mistakes, grammatical errors and general issues with response structure. In my view, this is the very least you should do if you want to be taken seriously. Show the assessor you respect their time and the grant funding process.

Preparation is key. The biggest, most important aspect of asking for a peer review is to make it as easy as possible for the reviewer to review. Supply all the information they will need to provide insightful feedback. That means sharing the funding program guidelines, links to program FAQs and any support information you're proposing to include with the application, such as a pitch video or product summary.

Ask them about:

- Reading speed;
- Narrative and story arc; and
- Feeling confidence through your words.

Any and all feedback will add value to the application and improve your chances of being funded, even if it's a confirmation that you can stand by what you've written. It's not necessary to take on all the suggested feedback. It may be that you disagree with some comments, but it serves to help tighten responses or plug a gap in your communication.

It's really about being extra rigorous. Can you defend your application from every angle? Are there things you haven't thought about or that could be ambiguous?

In the name of reciprocity

Don't be that person who calls on others but never makes yourself available to support peers when they've got an application or submission.

Time is always precious, as anyone growing a business knows. Helping a colleague with a peer review will also deliver benefits to you because every review you do, you'll notice something really cool about how others interpret questions or present responses.

Every time you give, I guarantee you'll receive something beneficial in return.

Advanced Grant Writing Action

In preparation for your next or your first grant application, take a moment now to make a list of trusted people you could call on as peer reviewers.

Be sure to note the criteria you might want to consider when deciding whom to ask. It is a crucial step in the process and shouldn't be just anyone!

In the meantime, if you know of someone who is working on an application, offer to review it for them. Start with giving your time first, as it will help fine-tune your appreciation of the selection criteria for when it is your turn.

It really is the easiest action of all.

Just in time for the end of the book!

THIS IS NOT THE END

You're only just beginning!

Congratulations, you've made it to the end of this book, but guess what … this is the start of a brand new experience, seeking and securing funding!

Whilst a grant application might have the primary purpose of securing external funding, I promise that the process of completing an application will also help you become a more informed entrepreneur with enhanced ability to grow a business that delivers legacy and stands the test of time!

The knowledge you've acquired throughout *Advanced Grant Writing for Female Founders* will hold you in safe hands for many years to come.

Sure, grant programs will evolve to focus on outcomes that are meaningful and specific to the funders responsible for establishing the program, but what you've learned here is adaptable and flexible and can be applied in many different situations.

For example, Section 1 focused on understanding the grant program, its objectives and proposed outcomes, and in so doing it will also help you to identify potential partnership opportunities. You now have the ability to identify what is valuable information, why it is important and how it applies to you as an entrepreneur, as well as to your business.

Section 2 of the book broke down a grant application, section by section, and analysed questions which helped you look for critical clues to draft responses that effectively narrated your business story and its successes.

Then, Section 3 lifted the curtain on the world of grant assessment by permitting you to step into the shoes of an assessor. Moving forward the assessment process shared will help you to take an objective look at your draft responses, and identify areas that are naturally strong, as well as opportunities for improvement that are as yet untapped.

And finally, Section 4 held the secrets to adding polish and pizzazz to your application responses, to leverage digital tools, and to build structure into your planning by staying on top of due dates and deadlines.

Here you are

I'm quietly confident that you've experienced a whole spectrum of *the feels* along this journey. But here you are, exactly where you need to be. More informed about the world of grant funding and absolutely ready. Ready to take the next step in advancing your business goals. If you want an extra $15,000 to kick start the testing of a new offer in a new market, fab! You know how to position your business to secure it! If you're ready for more – say, $50,000 – to start a pilot program testing the rollout of your new distribution and pricing model, amazing! You've got the foundations of your plan built, and the extension will be easy.

Right now, in this moment of time, you know exactly what is required of your business to be ready to apply for $100,000 *or more* in funding business growth. You've got the insight and the tools to smash it!

It's not one-and-done ...

With every grant application you complete and submit for consideration, you will refine and improve your responses. By the very nature of the process, you will receive feedback that builds on the previous. It's like day one of a 30-day personalised health and well-being program. The first day you are feeling stiff and out-of-sorts. But as the days progress you receive feedback and adjust your actions to arrive at the end feeling stronger and more confident than when you started. But do you stop? No way! You continue. Either with an intention to maintain the level you achieved, or to continue improving.

Here's the thing ... it doesn't matter if your goal is improving your health and well-being or applying for your first grant, you've got to take the first step. Committing to completing your first application, having it reviewed and submitted is just the catalyst you need to embed an evolving process of business improvement. And maybe you will even be successful in securing funding from your first application. I was, so why not you?

The possibilities are endless

My recommendation is that you keep a record of everything you prepare each time you complete a draft application. That way, you'll have copies of the market calculations you used for the first application which can be used to build upon in later applications. Evidence of market-product-fit can be expanded as your success statistics improve over time.

You might also find that different pieces of the application can be used on your website, in partnership proposals, when preparing competition or award submissions, or even as marketing content.

The time you allocate to your $100,000 application can also be leveraged to support your growth planning, sales forecasts, and future budget allocations. As I said above, the possibilities really are endless.

I'll be here, cheering you on and helping where I can, continuing to empower women entrepreneurs, one grant opportunity at a time.

PLEASE TAKE A MOMENT TO LEAVE A REVIEW

If you enjoyed the book and found it valuable, I would be incredibly grateful if you could take a few moments to share your thoughts by leaving a review on Amazon. Your feedback can make a significant difference for other potential readers and means a lot to me personally.

To leave a review, you can follow these steps:

Go to the book's page on Amazon;

Scroll down to the Customer Reviews section; and

Click on the "Write a customer review" button.

Even just a few lines about your experience of the book can have an impact. If for any reason the book didn't meet your expectations, please feel free to let me know directly. Your feedback helps me grow as an author.

Thank you once again for your support. It means the world to me.

Glossary

Term	Definition
Accelerator	Is usually a highly selective, intensive program that offers funding, mentorship, education and networking necessary to jump-start growth. Typically in exchange for equity in the company.
Acquittal	An acquittal is the process of evaluating and reporting on outcomes and expenditure of grant funds provided. The report might be collated by an independent auditor or prepared by an accountant. It will be requested at the conclusion of the project to confirm that the funding has been used for the purpose outlined in the funding application.
Award	An acknowledgment for business achievement generally in a defined category such as social impact, environment impact or the like. May sometimes include cash rewards.
Business	A mechanism to provide a product or service in exchange for a financial return.
Business Incentive Grant	A type of financial assistance package provided by governments or private organisations to encourage or support specific business activities, projects or investments. These grants are designed to stimulate economic development, job creation, innovation and other strategic goals that benefit the local or national economy.

Capital - External	Money raised external to the business, often from debt funders or investors or company shareholders.
Capital - Internal	Money generated by the business, usually from sales revenue, not distributed to shareholders.
Co-Contribution	A financial arrangement where the recipient of a grant is required to contribute a portion of the funding towards the project or initiative being supported.
	The granting organisation then matches or supplements this contribution with their own funds. This means that both parties, the grant recipient and the granting organisation, collaborate by providing financial resources to achieve a common goal.
Collaboration	Working with another business to produce or deliver on a shared goal.
Commercialisation	The process of taking a product, technology or innovation from the research and development phase to market for sale or widespread use. It involves turning an idea or concept into a commercially viable product or service that can be sold to consumers, businesses or other end-users.
Competition	A competition will often award, recognise and reward outstanding businesses whose passion, determination, and innovation deliver stand-out results. May sometimes include cash rewards.
Convertible Note	This type of debt can be converted into equity (e.g. shares of stock) at a later date, providing flexibility for the founder.
Debt-Financing	A method of raising capital for a business by borrowing money from external sources, such as banks, financial institutions, or investors, with the promise to repay the principal amount along with interest over a specified period of time. This type of financing allows businesses to access funds without giving up ownership stakes (equity).

Types of Debt-Financing	• Bank loans • Corporate bonds • Lines of Credit • Trade Credit • Convertible Debt (or Note)
ETFs	Exchange Traded Fund – pooled investment fund, similar to a traditional managed fund, but which can be bought or sold like any share on the stock exchange.
Entity	A formal, legally recognised structure that underpins an operating business. It defines how your business is set up, who owns it, how it's managed and how it's taxed.
Entity Types	• Sole Proprietor (Sole Trader) • Partnership • Joint Venture (JV) • Limited Liability Company (LLC) • Limited Liability Partnership (LLP) • Incorporated Corporation/Company (PTY LTD) • B Corp (Benefit Corporation) • Non-Profit Corporation • Charitable Incorporated Organisation (CIO) • Cooperative • Trust • Unicorporated Association
Equity	Equity refers to ownership interest or a stake that an individual or entity holds in a company or asset. In simpler terms, it's what remains for the owners (or shareholders) after all debts and obligations are settled.
Equity-Free Funding	Equity-free funding refers to financial support provided to a business or project without requiring the recipient to give up any ownership stake or equity in return. In other words, the funding does not involve exchanging shares of the company or project for the investment. Instead, the recipient retains full ownership and control.

Equity-Free Funding - Types	• Grants • Contests or Competitions • Accelerator and Incubator Programs • Crowdfunding • Prizes and Fellowships • Corporate Sponsorship and Partnerships
Funder	Person or organisation with funding on offer.
Founder	The person who establishes the business or organisation. They are the person who kickstarts the venture, usually originating from an idea or concept created by the same person.
Growth Grant	A type of funding product provided to businesses, typically by government agencies or private organisations, to support their expansion, development, and growth initiatives. Unlike loans, grants do not need to be repaid.
Incubator	If an Accelerators help you to 'accelerate' an existing business process, an Incubator helps those with an innovative idea further develop it.
Investment Vehicle	An investment vehicle is a specialised method investors use to invest their money. It is a method of investing or a platform used to invest funds, in a way that is tailored to the investor's financial goals, risk tolerance and preferences.
Investment Vehicles - Types of	Direct Investment = stocks, bonds or real estate Indirect categorised as = Private or Public • Public = Mutual Funds or ETFs • Private = Venture Capital
Joint Venture (JV)	A joint venture is a business arrangement where two or more independent entities come together to collaborate on a specific project, venture, or business activity. In a joint venture, these entities pool their resources, expertise and capital to achieve a common goal.
Partnerships	Collaborations, joint ventures with other businesses/organisations with aligned and/or complementary goals.

Priority Groups	Often defined by a Funder or a grant program management team as 'groups' of applicants considered to be favoured over others because of their assigned priority status.
Publicly Listed Company	A publicly listed company, also known as a publicly traded company or a public company, is a corporation whose ownership shares are available for purchase by the general public on a stock exchange. This means that anyone, including individuals, institutional investors and other companies, can buy and sell shares of the company.
Startup	An early-stage, innovative or disruptive business that is scalable and is either working on a new or novel product/service and/or has devised a different business model.
Scalable	A startup that can grow quickly and has the potential to address large national and international markets, including the ability to (easily) enter new markets.
Unencumbered	Refers to an asset or property that is free and clear of any liens, claims or restrictions. It means that the asset is wholly owned by an individual or entity, and there are no legal or financial obligations attached to it.
Venture Capital (VC)	Venture capital is a form of private investment where individuals or firms provide funding to early-stage or startup companies in exchange for ownership equity or a stake in the business. This capital is typically used to support the growth and development of young companies, often in high-potential industries like technology or biotechnology. Venture capitalists, or VC firms, take calculated risks on startups with the expectation of achieving substantial returns if the company succeeds and eventually goes public or is acquired.

Acknowledgments

The women who have supported and inspired my journey

In acknowledgment of the love and support I've received during my time in this gracious, magical, delightful earth experience, I pay tribute to the women in my life who have impacted me profoundly, both personally and professionally.

First and foremost, a massive thank you to Kris Emery. Not only had I never written a book before, but I had never considered working with a professional editor. It blows my mind just how easy and enjoyable the process of writing has been. You provided the structure I needed, whilst allowing me flexibility to *just go with the flow*. You knew just what to say, at the right time. Your words of encouragement helped me to believe that I could achieve this amazing milestone. It took longer than expected, but I think that's a good thing! Can't wait to get going on the next one.

My dearest friends Karin and Nicole. You've been my cheerleaders throughout the years, encouraging me when I felt clueless about what it meant to author a book – let alone a book designed to help women get funded. No biggie.

Nicole, you opened your New Zealand home to me and gave me the freedom to immerse myself in a beautiful environment that provided natural inspiration. There, I wrote a draft framework for what ultimately evolved into this book. Karin, you provided an unwavering belief in me and the gift of your time in completing the final checks before printing. I feel so humbled by the generosity you've both offered. Thank you.

Credit for book cover design and formatting is due, with thanks, to Hazel Lam. What a talent you are and how lucky am I that you had capacity to take on this little project. I look at what you've done and can hardly believe it is my book!

Alix and Melissa, thank you for your listening ears, letting me ramble on in awe of this process and about what I learned along the way.

My son, Lachlan, for picking up the slack around home. Preparing meals, letting me sleep in after a late, late night and vacating the apartment so I wouldn't be disturbed. Your thoughtfulness and care when I became, at times, totally self-absorbed was incredible. You understood how important this activity was to me and to the women I am writing for. Thank you.

One last thank you – to you, the women who heard the call and stepped forward with bravery and courage to take up the challenge of becoming an entrepreneur.

The world needs more leaders like you … leaders growing successful, financially sustainable businesses because a thriving business gives power to the women who grow them.

Thank you for stepping into the arena with me.

About the Author

Lisa Erhart - Funding Specialist and Advocate for Women Entrepreneurs

About Lisa:

Meet Lisa Erhart, a passionate funding specialist with over two decades of experience dedicated to helping women entrepreneurs and business owners secure the external funding they need to scale and grow their businesses. With a wealth of knowledge gained through her own remarkable journey in the funding arena, Lisa is on a mission to empower women to achieve their own funded success.

Experience and Accomplishments:

In her remarkable journey, Lisa accomplished what many aspire to achieve in a short span of time. As an applicant, she secured an impressive $2.4 million in funding within just 18 months, a feat that would ultimately grow to an astounding $4.2 million. Beyond her success as an applicant, Lisa has played a pivotal role in assessing over $50 million in applications submitted to government funding programs and private funds.

A Unique Perspective:

What sets Lisa apart is her ability to view the funding landscape from both sides. Her expertise and the innovative programs she develops stem from her unique perspective, encompassing both the roles of an applicant and an assessor. Lisa's firsthand knowledge equips her with invaluable insights into the highly competitive funding environment, especially where female founders are often overlooked and undervalued.

Harnessing Collective Power:
Lisa believes that when women come together, they tap into a collective power that has the potential to ignite innovative and sustainable change. Her role is to help you harness your own unique blend of determination and drive, guiding you to secure the funding required to nurture a financially sustainable business that leaves a lasting impact on the world.

Connect with Lisa:
If you'd like to learn more about Lisa's funding journey, jump across to the www.funding4growth.io website and download Lisa's Funding Roadmap, found on the About Us page. It's where she details, step by step, the process she undertook to secure millions of dollars in funding.

Here's the URL https://www.funding4growth.io/about-us

Scroll down to the opt-in box, and you'll have immediate access.

Find Lisa Online

I love connecting with entrepreneurs looking for funding to grow businesses that have impact and set women up for long-term and sustainable financial success. Get in touch anytime through the socials.

Like my page on Facebook:
https://www.facebook.com/Funding4Growth

Follow me on Instagram:
https://www.instagram.com/funding4growth/

Subscribe to my channel on YouTube:
https://www.youtube.com/@funding4growth

Visit the website for more:
https://www.funding4growth.io/

Get More Support

When you're ready to take the next step to funding your business growth, you'll find additional resources available on my website.

Maybe you're not yet ready to apply for $100,000 or more? That's okay, I've prepared a guide to help you source $5,000 or $10,000 grants. Start small and work your way up to larger amounts.

https://www.funding4growth.io/em-grants

Included in my bio is a link to download my Funding Roadmap, but if you're looking for a guide that includes broader funding options that align with the commercialisation pathway, then download it from my website.

https://www.funding4growth.io/roadmap

Prepare to take your grant application to the next level, whether it's your first time or you're aiming for another successful grant win. We've got you covered with our exclusive *Funding Application Essentials* bundle. Click the link below to access a comprehensive set of templates that will supercharge your documentation and set you on the path to funded success.

https://www.funding4growth.io/ap-essentials

If you've loved this book and would like to leverage what you've learned by participating in an Advanced Grant Writing Challenge facilitated by me, you'll find more information on my website.

https://www.funding4growth.io/agw-challenge

When a brain is stretched with the learning of a new concept or acquisition of new knowledge, it can never revert back to where it started. In the process of acquiring the new knowledge, neurons fire, neural pathways are created, and the brain's ability to adapt and change is enhanced. That is the power of neuroplasticity.

So it is for your business.

Let's call it EntrepreneurialPlasticity.

Manufactured by Amazon.com.au
Sydney, New South Wales, Australia

16108967R00121